DIALOGUE JOURNAL WRITING WITH NONNATIVE ENGLISH SPEAKERS: A HANDBOOK FOR TEACHERS

JOY KREEFT PEYTON
LESLEE REED

Typeset in Aster and Helvetica
by World Composition Services, Inc., Sterling, Virginia
and printed by Pantagraph Printing, Bloomington, Illinois

Director of Publications: Helen Kornblum
Publications Assistant: Rosanna Landis

Library of Congress Catalog No. 89-051727
ISBN 0-939791-37-4

CONTENTS

Preface vii

Chapter 1
Dialogue journals in the classroom:
A reflection by Leslee Reed 1

Chapter 2
What is a dialogue journal? 3
    Variations on the basic journal format 10

Chapter 3
What are the benefits of dialogue journal writing?...........13
    There are increased opportunities for communica-
        tion between students and teachers 13
    The teacher can individualize language and content
        learning 18
    The teacher gains information that can assist in
        lesson planning 25
    Students have the opportunity to use writing for
        genuine communication......................................27
    Students have an additional opportunity for reading 32
    Some words of caution 33

Chapter 4
Using dialogue journals with different kinds of students 35
    Beginning writers..37
    Literate writers...46
    More advanced writers 51

Chapter 5
Getting started 57
    What to write in 47
    With whom to write..58
    How often to write 58

When to write 59
How much to write 59
Introducing the idea 59

Chapter 6

Keeping it going: Strategies for maintaining the dialogue 61
Keeping the conversation going 61
Finding time for the dialogue 64
Correcting the writing 65
Finding topics to write about 66
Keeping the writing from becoming too personal 67
Maintaining privacy...68

Chapter 7

What to do if . . . ?: Strategies for handling problems.................69
Writing with the reluctant writer 69
Writing with the repetitive writer 71
Writing with the student who has "nothing to write
    about"...72
Responding to entries that are difficult to decipher 73
Addressing behavior problems 75
Responding to angry entries 78
Writing in the student's native language 79

Chapter 8

Profiles of individual student writers...............................81
Catalina: Starting with drawing 81
Miguel: The development of English fluency 95
Larry: The defeated student who blossomed 99
Janny: The "good student" and the development of a
    voice 100

Chapter 9

**Conclusion: Studying dialogue journal writing:
A reflection by Joy Peyton** 109

References...113
Appendix: Further reading 119

ACKNOWLEDGMENTS

So many students and teachers have contributed to this handbook, by opening their classrooms and journals to us and talking with us freely about their experiences with journals, that it is impossible to mention them all. Many are mentioned specifically in the text; others are not named, or are given pseudonyms. We are grateful to all of you.

Jana Staton has been an inspiration throughout the creation of this handbook. She encouraged us to write it in the first place, helped us to formulate our thoughts and clarify them as we proceeded, and read and commented on numerous drafts.

We appreciate the ongoing support for this project and very helpful comments on earlier drafts from many fellow dialogue journal users, researchers, and interested colleagues; in particular, Donna Christian, Shelley Gutstein, Etta Johnson, Paul Jones, Carolyn Kessler, and Lila Silverman. The final version has benefited greatly from the comments of Ann Raimes, Rosanna Landis, and two anonymous TESOL reviewers.

A large part of this work was supported by a grant to the Center for Language Education and Research (CLEAR) from the Office of Educational Research and Improvement (OERI) of the U.S. Department of Education.

PREFACE

Dialogue journals are a versatile tool that can be used in any classroom, with students of any age, from early elementary to adult. In this handbook we focus on nonnative English speaking students, at elementary through high school levels, but most of the points covered are applicable to other populations as well—adult students learning English as a second language (ESL) or dialect, students learning a foreign language, or native English-speaking students writing in English. The discussion and examples should give ample information to any teacher desiring to use dialogue journals with students of any age. We hope that dialogue journal writing proves to be as enjoyable and productive for you as it has been for us!

Joy Kreeft Peyton and Leslee Reed

DIALOGUE JOURNALS
IN THE CLASSROOM

A Reflection by Leslee Reed

Every student who starts school faces the unknown—a new teacher, a new situation, new classmates—and wonders, "How will I get along in this situation?" First day jitters are common, even for those who have attended the same school for a number of years. Imagine then, the heightened emotional impact of a new school year for students from other countries, who cannot speak the language, are not sure of the customs, and may even fear for their safety. Being laughed at by others, not being understood, or even needing to use the restroom and being too embarrassed to ask can create emotional stress for new non-English speaking students.

After the first days of school, once they have developed some assurance that the teacher, classroom, and fellow classmates are safe and that there are ways of coping, students are usually ready to talk to someone, to express their fear or confusion, and to ask for explanations about new customs, behaviors, and classroom activities. The teacher is the obvious person to turn to, but attempting to talk to the teacher can be frustrating. After working up the courage to approach the teacher, and despite careful mental rehearsals, students often feel uncertain of what to say, or find that someone else is there listening in, or that the teacher responds with a question or comment which the student doesn't understand. The result can be a renewed sense of failure, which can eventually undermine the willingness to attempt to communicate at all. Dialogue journals can ease the pain of such face-to-face encounters by providing a nonthreatening way for students to communicate.

My own experience with using dialogue journals has convinced me

1

that students who come to the classroom unable to speak English soon find that the journals can be a real source of comfort and satisfaction. Each day my students find messages written specifically for them. They have a sense of personal identity and a personal link with me. They can ask for help in the journal, and no one will laugh at them for asking "dumb questions." The journal is the one area in which the students in my mainstream classroom who come from other countries and are learning English can participate as equals with those who have been in this country all of their lives. Like all students, they read and write in their journal each day. Incorrect spelling and grammar do not make a difference in the journals; the message is the important thing. The students know that I "hear" them, and they respond even if they are unable to speak out orally. No one laughs at their mistakes, and incorrect usage of words is not noted or ridiculed.

When my students arrive at school each morning, they head straight for their dialogue journals. They know I have given my attention to them and to them alone through my written response. They understand what I have written to them because the words, structures, and ideas are designed to be those words, structures, and ideas needed most at their stage of development—not repetitive drills of words and structures that have no meaning for them.

As the days pass, my students learn that they can communicate their ideas, and they become more and more aware of how English words and sentences fit together. They also develop confidence that they are accepted. How important these feelings are to any learner! And how much more to the student learning English.

CHAPTER 2

WHAT IS A DIALOGUE JOURNAL?

The use of this [reciprocal interaction] model in teaching requires a genuine dialogue between student and teacher in both oral and written modalities, guidance and facilitation rather than control . . . by the teacher. . . . This model emphasizes . . . meaningful language use by students rather than the correction of surface forms.

Jim Cummins, 1986, p. 28

. . . what the teacher must be, to be an effective competence model, is a day-to-day working model with whom to interact. It is not so much that the teacher provides a model to imitate. Rather, it is that the teacher can become a part of the student's internal dialogue— somebody whose respect he wants, someone whose standards he wishes to make his own. It is like becoming a speaker of a language one shares with somebody. The language of that interaction becomes a part of oneself, and the standards of style and clarity that one adopts for that interaction become a part of one's own standards.

Jerome Bruner, 1966, p. 124

A dialogue journal, put very simply, is a conversation between a teacher and an individual student. However, this conversation differs from all others they may have, in or out of the classroom; it is written, it is completely private, and it takes place regularly and continually throughout an entire school year or semester. All that is required is a bound notebook and a teacher who is interested in what students have to say and committed to writing regularly to each of them. Students write regularly in the journal, as much as they want and about whatever they choose, and the teacher writes back—not grading or correcting the writing, and not responding with simple platitudes or evaluative comments such as "Good!" or "Interesting point!" The teacher is a *partner* in a conversation, who accepts what is written and responds as directly and openly as possible, while keeping in mind the student's language ability and interests. The value of the dialogue journal lies in the open exchange of ideas that can occur and the concerned and warm acceptance by the teacher of the student's writing. Daily exchange of the journal is ideal, as the continuity of writing and immediacy of a response keeps a flow of ideas going and makes responding much easier and quicker for the teacher. If it is not possible to write and respond daily, it is crucial that the writing take place regularly, at least twice a week. Many teachers find it beneficial to write each time the student writes to maintain the sense of dialogue and avoid the sense of more formal, composed writing. Other teachers, who do not respond to each student entry, at least write regularly.

Let's "listen in" on the written dialogues between Leslee Reed and two of her sixth grade students who are at different stages of learning English as a second language. The first exchange is with Michael, a Burmese student, who wrote this entry 10 months after he began attending school in the United States and learning English. [These examples and those throughout this handbook are drawn from the actual writing of teachers and students. In all cases the writing is reproduced as it was written, without changes to grammar, spelling, or punctuation. Students' names are changed, except when they indicated that they wanted their real names to be used.]

February 9
> Michael: Mrs. Reed you know on this week like the silly week. I don't know what happen on this week. Mrs. Reed what did you mean about the valentines you said we have to bring the valentines. Did we have to made the valentines for ~~people~~ our classroom. I didn't know what are you talking.

> Mrs. Reed: No, you don't have to give anyone a Valentine. It is just fun to do. Sometimes we like someone but we do not tell them. We feel funny telling someone you really like them. Giving a Valentine is an easy way of doing it. If you want to give a valentine or 5 valentines—it doesn't matter. You do what you want about that.

February 10
> Michael: Mrs. Reed I know what is the valentine but I don't know what I have to do and the valentine is we have to give the cards to someone and we I have to buy the cards but I can't buy the cards thats is the problems. I think I'm

not going to the sofeball because I did not do nothing about it and Ricardo said I could be the catcher and he break his primise.

Mrs. Reed: No problem! Anyone who wants to give valentines can. If you don't want to give valentines you don't have to.

Talk to Ricardo again! I'm sure he forgot his promise when others on the team began yelling at him.

Did you ever find your pen?

February 11

Michael: I didn't not find my pen. Happy Valentine! I want to give the cards to people but I can't give the cards to people. I give the one card to the simon. I think Level 10 hard me. Did you think Level 10 is hard for me? I saw the Thanksgiving Pilgrim in the book. You know, today morning U Chal put cards in every bag except Tony. I know why U Chal put the cards every card because he put cards into every bag so that he margar him. You said we are going to do the art with the shoe box, and you said you don't have the shoe box you can't do art.

Mrs. Reed: I am not sure what you said. U Chal put cards in everyone's sack so they don't *margar* him. What word did you put there? Please tell me.

Yes, we will do the shoebox art. Everyone who has a shoebox will do it. Have a happy vacation. I will see you in five days.

The second exchange is with Claudia, who is from El Salvador and had been in the United States for two and a half years when these entries were written.

March 17

Claudia: The new teacher or helper in our class is very good. I like her, don't you like her? Today she helped me & us a lot. I was just going to get down to get something she would get it for everyone. I hope she stays with us the whole year until the end. Tony didn't want any help though. Why doesn't Tony want us to help him?

I will try & bring my lunch every day from now on because the turkey stew & other lunches put me sick. I hate them. When I am very hungry I have to eat them but when I get to my house my stomach hurts & I am sick for 3 days. Can't the teachers protest or say something about the food that they give here?

              What do you feed chickens here? We have a hen that layd & egg.

Mrs. Reed: The lunches are not that bad! I've eaten them sometimes. You are wise to bring your own lunch. That is usually what I do, too. Today some people ate 3 lunches—so they must have liked them. You have such good food at home that nothing served here could taste so good!

              Tony is embarrassed. He wants help, but he does not want anyone to know that he needs it. Offer to help him and if he says "no" then leave him alone.

              Chickens will eat scraps of bread, wheat, seeds, water and some insects.

March 18

Claudia: Oh but the hen has some white lines in her dirt of her body that throws up by a hole. I don't know what you call it. She has wat it looks like worms, but little worms those white ugly worms & they are very skiny, what are they? do you know how to get the hen of her stomach sickness or is it usual for her to be like that because she is laying eggs and she could even lay 30 eggs so I do not know if it is usual or if it is a sickness of her.

              oh poor hen she cooks & coocks when I say pretty hen in a low low voice & she looks like she is used to children because she is cook & cooking when I say pretty things, oh she's so nice!!!!

Mrs. Reed: It is normal for the feces (the waste from your hen's body) to have white lines in it. I've never heard of a hen having worms—but it is possible. Go to a pet shop and ask them or to a veterinarian. Who gave you the hen, maybe they will know.

              We say that a hen clucks. It is a pleasant little sound as though they are happy. They cackle when they lay an egg! That is usually loud! Does your hen cackle?

              I think hens like having people or other hens around, don't you?

Claudia: Yes I like & she likes people around her & when I talk she kinds of understands & when she doesn't she kind of looks up so I can tell her again whatever I told her & and then she understands me, oh you should see her. Maybe in the future I will bring it to school then we could study her & see how she is, looks, & how she eats, don't you think it would be a great idea, (I do).

Figures 1 and 2 show parts of these dialogues as they appeared in the journals.

In studies of dialogue journal writing in two of Mrs. Reed's sixth grade classes, one made up of native English speakers (Staton, Shuy, Peyton, & Reed, 1988) and the other, of nonnative English speakers (Kreeft, Shuy, Staton, Reed, & Morroy, 1984), we identified the following characteristics of the interaction, illustrated by the above examples:

- *The writing has the qualities of good conversation.* Both the students and the teacher can choose topics to discuss. Both can contribute equally, making comments and offering observations and opinions; requesting and giving clarification; asking and answering questions.
- *The writing is student-generated.* Because the students write before the teacher each day, they generally write about activities they are involved in and issues that interest them, as they happen. The teacher also initiates topics, but most often responds to the students' topics, supporting and encouraging their writing. Therefore, the teacher essentially shares control of the writing with the students (see also Peyton & Seyoum, 1989).
- *The writing is continual.* The daily journal exchange allows students to discuss certain topics with their teacher over a period of several days, weeks, or even months, such as the discussion of Valentine cards in Michael's entries and the hen in Claudia's entries. It is not necessary to say everything about a topic in one entry, and over time the writers begin to build on each other's thoughts, words, and manners of self-expression. Other topics might be introduced as they arise, discussed, and dropped when they are no longer important, e.g., the question about Michael's pen or Claudia's comments about the new teacher.
- *The writing is functional.* Students write to accomplish a wide variety of real purposes. They might request information (Claudia—"What do you feed chickens here?"), an opinion (Michael—"Did you think Level 10 is hard for me?"), or clarification (Michael—"What did you mean about the valentines?"); offer an opinion (Claudia—"The new teacher or helper in our class is very good. I like her . . ."); describe a personal problem

Figure 1

Feb. 9

Mrs. Reed you know on this week like the silly week. I don't know what happen on this week. Mrs. Reed what did you mean about the valentines you said we have to bring the valentimes. Did we have to made the valentines for people our classroom. I dint know what are you talking.

No, you don't have to give anyone a Valentine. It is just a fun thing to do. Sometimes we like someone but we do not tell them. We feel funny telling someone you really like them. Giving a Valentine is an easy way of doing it. If you want to give a valentine or 50 valentines -- it doesn't matter. You do what you want about that.

Figure 2

Oh poor hen she cooks & cooks, when I say pretty hen in a low low voice & she looks like she is used to children because she is cook & cooking when I say pretty things, oh she's so nice!!!

Mar. 18

It is normal for the feces (the waste from your hen's body) to have white lines in it. I've never heard of a hen having worms -- but it is possible. Go to a pet shop and ask them or to a veterinarian. Who gave you the hen, maybe they will know.

(Michael—"we have to give the cards to someone, and I have to buy the card, but I can't buy the cards thats is the problems"); or express a complaint (Michael—"Ricardo says I could be the catcher and he break his promise."; Claudia—"the turkey stew & other lunches put me sick. I hate them.").

- *The writing is varied in terms of topic, genre, and length.* Although students are usually allowed to write about personal topics, they may also be encouraged to discuss nonpersonal topics, such as things they are studying in school, books they are reading, or current events. They may write descriptions, explanations, narratives, complaints, or arguments with supporting details, as the topic and communicative purposes dictate. Entries or topics may be as brief as a few sentences, or they may extend for several pages.

Variations on the Basic Journal Format

This handbook focuses primarily on one particular type of dialogue journal writing—a student-teacher conversation, handwritten and contained in a bound notebook, in which students write about topics of their own choosing. However, many variations on this basic format for interactive writing are possible and are being used effectively as well. These might involve varying the participants, the content of the writing, or the type of journal used.

Participants in the dialogue

The dialogue journal partner does not have to be the teacher. Students can write with a classroom aide, a pairing which can be especially helpful if the aide knows the students' native language, and they can begin writing in that language. Students at upper elementary or secondary levels might be paired with each other. Nancie Atwell's (1984, 1987) junior high school students write to each other as well as to her about literature they are reading. Students just beginning to learn English might be paired with those who are more proficient, or students in one class might be paired with older students in another class. Heath and Branscombe, 1984, describe interactive writing between 9th and 12th grade students. Dialogue journal partners can be anyone who has the desire, time, and skills to keep the interaction going. They might be researchers working with the class (described in Heath & Branscombe, 1984; Samway, 1989), parents, or retired persons who want to become involved with the life of the school.

Journal content

Rather than leaving dialogue journal topics completely open-ended, the teacher might want to focus the discussion on course content. Taylor (1988), Atwell (1984, 1987), Steffensen (1988), and Walworth (1985; 1990), report their successful use of dialogue journals in literature classes (with upper elementary, junior high, and college students) in which students use their journals to discuss books they are reading. Taylor's students also write with an outside researcher, with whom they share drafts of their writing and talk about their writing in progress (Samway, 1989). Journals can also be used in social studies, science, history, and math classes, providing a place for reflecting on course content, relating content to personal experience, and talking things over with another person who is immersed in the same classroom content (Borasi & Rose, in press; Rose, 1989; see also articles in *Dialogue*, September, 1989). Likewise, prospective teachers in teacher training courses reflect with their professors about their new experiences and growth as teachers (Brinton & Holten, 1989; Roderick, 1986; Roderick & Berman, 1984; see also *Dialogue*, September, 1988). It is best, however, not to control the topic for discussion too tightly. Sometimes students simply need a place to air thoughts and feelings, even those which are not directly related to the focus of study.

Type of journal

The dialogue need not be written in a notebook at all. In classes with word processors that are easily accessible to all students, the "journal" may be on a disk passed back and forth. Entries are saved on the disk, just as they would be saved in a notebook, and printed out from time to time. Special software for keeping a dialogue journal, called *Dialog Maker*, is available as well (cf. Sayers, 1986a). With this software the teacher can combine general and individual messages to students, thus saving teacher writing time. If schools have access to electronic mail, messages can be sent without the exchange of disks.

With access to computer conferencing networks such as *Bitnet* or *The Source*, students can keep dialogue journals with other students across the United States or even in different parts of the world. The speed of electronic mail gives pen pal correspondence the immediacy of the dialogue journal (cf. Naiman, 1988; Sayers, 1986b). Another format is that of the oral dialogue journal, in which students and a teacher, or nonnative and native English speaking students, exchange cassette tapes. (See MacDonald, 1989, for a description.)

One essential feature of these journals is that they be a *dialogue*. Recently the practice of journal writing has become a standard part of the curriculum of many programs. Upon hearing about dialogue journals, some teachers say, "I've been doing that for years." What they are actually using, though, are personal journals, logs, or diaries, in which students write, but the teacher doesn't respond, beyond a few brief comments about the students' writing. A true dialogue requires that both parties make substantive contributions of more or less equal length and discuss some topics of mutual interest.

Whatever the variations in journal type, the basic features, principles, and strategies for dialogue journal writing are the same. Students have the opportunity to use writing to communicate: to express concepts that are important to them, to accomplish real purposes, to be read by an interested audience, and to receive a reply that is genuine and meaningful.

CHAPTER 3

WHAT ARE THE BENEFITS OF DIALOGUE JOURNAL WRITING?

There are no shy students in the dialogue journal. Reluctant speakers are among my most eager writers. A Vietnamese girl who has tremendous difficulty with pronunciation and never speaks unless called upon writes long and meaningful entries in her journal. One day recently she wrote a beautifully constructed story. I was able to dispel another teacher's concern that she might have plagiarized a paper written for his class by demonstrating with her journal (after I had obtained her permission to share her writing) that her written work is far more sophisticated than her oral production would suggest.

Harriet L. Hulings, 9th–12th grade ESL teacher[1]

Teachers who use dialogue journals agree that their benefits are many and varied. We discuss here those benefits that are most frequently mentioned by experienced teachers.

There Are Increased Opportunities for Communication Between Students and Teachers

I enjoy using dialogue journals because it helps me learn about the kids. I see a side of the kids that I can never see in class, because they talk to me and tell me about what they're doing and how they feel.

Juanita Zientara, 9th–12th grade ESL teacher[2]

---

[1] From a paper written for a graduate course for ESL teachers.

[2] This and other quotes from teachers and students are taken from transcripts of extensive interviews conducted by Joy Peyton during the 1987–88 school year. We are grateful to Gina Richardson for combing these interviews for appropriate quotes.

I feel like I get to know the child better, and I can sometimes head off problems that might occur with students. If someone is having concerns about somebody else, I kind of work it around in the journals by writing to people, doing a little counseling.

Kelly Miller, 4th–6th grade ESL teacher

It's a way your teacher can get to know you better, and you can tell her your personal things. Like if you hurt or something, she'll listen. I mean, she'll read it and write back. . . . There are some people that always keep their thoughts inside; they never break out anything. But they can write it in the journal because the teacher won't tell anyone. And I think you can get those ideas out. Get them off your back and stuff.

11th grade ESL student

One of the most often-cited benefits of dialogue journal writing is the increased communication between students and teachers created and sustained throughout the school year. Since most teachers do not have time to converse at length with individual students each day, regular written interaction increases student-teacher contact time considerably. This time can be especially helpful in ESL pull-out programs, in which students are pulled from mainstream classes for special instruction in ESL, and the ESL teacher sees the students for only brief periods during a week. In dialogue journals students have the opportunity to express themselves openly and in private, without being embarrassed about the nature of their concerns or the limits of their language to express themselves. At the same time, the teacher can praise good work and offer encouragement or solace without embarrassing the student.

Many teachers have found that the dialogue journal interaction has a positive influence on their relationship with particular students. Some students, who tend to say very little in school, write prolifically in their dialogue journals. Without the journal, the teacher would know little or nothing about them. Other students, because of undesirable habits or behaviors, create a negative impression in face-to-face encounters and have difficulty with teachers and peers, but in the journal reveal a more appealing personality. They and the teacher can then find common ground on which to build a more positive relationship.

In the journal students can express their frustration with learning English, as Andy (a sixth grade student from Korea) does in the interaction below. The teacher then has the opportunity to provide support and encouragement. A reproduction of the interaction as it appeared in the journal is shown in Figure 3.

Figure 3

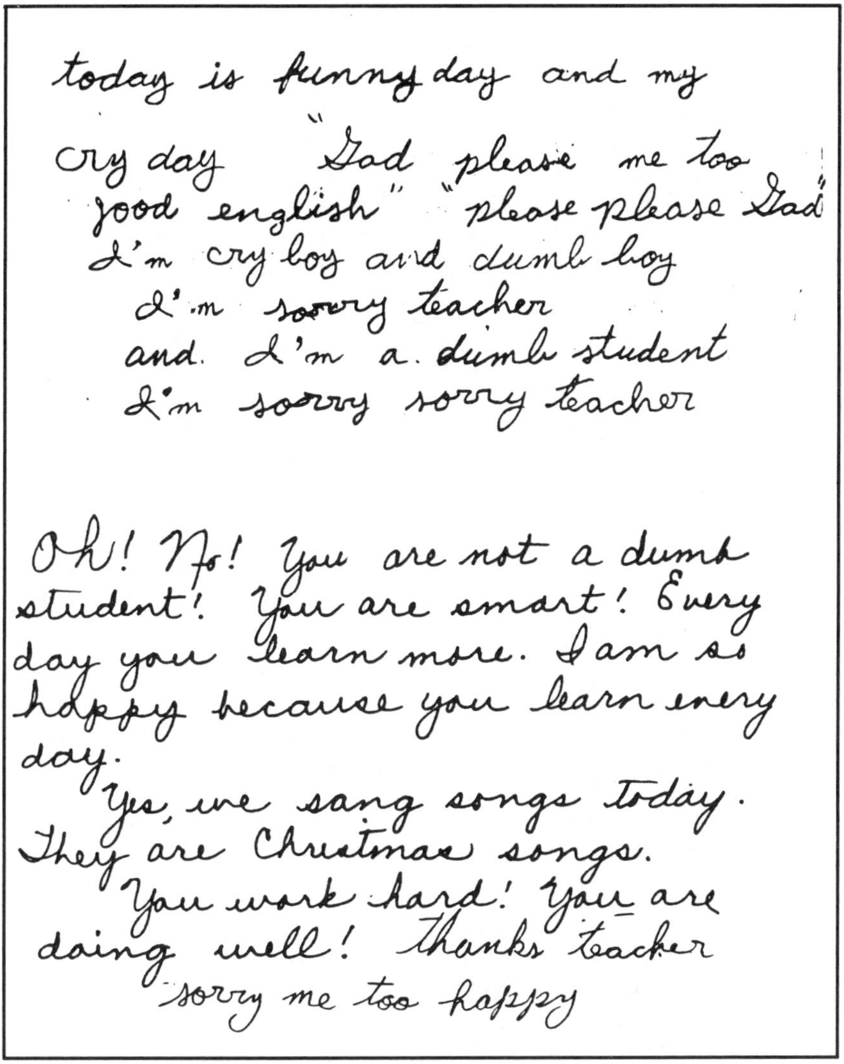

> today is funny day and my
> cry day "God please me too
> good english" "please please God"
> I'm cry boy and dumb boy
> I'm sorry teacher
> and. I'm a. dumb student
> I'm sorry sorry teacher
>
>
>
> Oh! No! You are not a dumb
> student! You are smart! Every
> day you learn more. I am so
> happy because you learn every
> day.
> Yes, we sang songs today.
> They are Christmas songs.
> You work hard! You are
> doing well! thanks teacher
> sorry me too happy

Andy: today is funny day and my cry day "God please me too good english" "please please God I'm cry boy and dumb boy I'm sorry teacher and I'm a dumb student I'm sorry sorry teacher

Teacher: Oh! No! You are not a dumb student! You are smart! Every day you learn more. I am so happy because you learn every day.

You work hard! You are doing well!

In addition to language problems, students who have recently arrived in the United States must deal with many other issues as they adjust to a new school and new culture and learn how to cope in their new situation. They may be lonely and mourning friends and relatives left behind in their country, or they and their families may be experiencing considerable trials in the transition process. In the journal they can write about their experiences and concerns, and the teacher has the chance to reply with empathy and understanding. In this interaction Andy explains that he is sad because his father is still in Korea, and he can't wish him a happy birthday.

> Andy: Today I am sorry my dad's birthday but I can't see, and I can't talk my dad so I am sorry to my dad.

> Teacher: It is too bad that you can't see your Dad, but it's great that you're writing him a letter in English. Would you like some help?

Tong, a young child in a refugee camp in Thailand on his way to the United States, writes about how much he misses his grandmother, who remains in Vietnam.

> Soon I will be in America so I will tell you about my grandmother who still lived in Vietnam. She lived in the island and had a big garden, mango trees and bamboo trees. She had many things. When I went there to visit her I was very happy. I loved my grandmother too much. She loved me, too. But when I escaped to Thailand I didn't say goodbye to her. Now maybe she is old and old. I think that she will miss me too much but I don't know when will I come back to see my grandmother again.

Students may also feel as if they are treated unfairly because of their cultural background. In the journal they can find a listening ear and some helpful advice. Juan, a 10th grade student from El Salvador, discusses his desire to be on the basketball team and his disappointment over not being accepted, and his teacher tries to explain why this might have happened.

> Juan: I will like very much to play in the school team of basketball. I will try to come to play after school. The problem is I don't know what to do for to bee part of a school team. I like to play basketball very much. In my country I played for my school team and I was a good player and I wish to play here too.

Teacher: Mr. B is the regular basketball coach. Do you know him? He is one of the counselors and an awfully nice person. If you are interested in basketball, he could tell you about the teams at school and how to try out.

Juan: I want to talk to Mr. B and he told me it is to late for to be in the team. I felt so sad and I steal sad. I would liked to play for the school, but the things are different. My friends told me the coach is very straight and he does a descrimination to the spanish people or chines. I thought that is very bad because that make me feel bad.

Teacher: I'm puzzled by this. I know Mr. B. very well, and I've seen him really work hard to help some of the Spanish-speaking students he has as counselor. There are several Spanish-speaking students on the team. I think you missed the deadline for tryouts. Why don't you ask some of the other students when the deadline for tryouts was to see if you really did miss it? Then next year, you can make sure that you try out for the team in time.

Students may have questions about the new culture that they do not feel free to ask in public. The journal gives them individualized access to a competent, adult member of the culture. Because the information they receive is in written form, students can refer back to it later. Here, Widianti, a 20-year-old student from Indonesia, in an adult ESL program, asks about etiquette when a guest in an American home.

Widianti: I have so many question—can you tell me, what usually people do if sombody invite them to live in their house for about 2 days—I mean what should they do in that house (of american people). Whats the polite and the impolite things that they can or can't do as a guest in that house. Mary asked me to come to her house and I am affraid so much—because I didn't know what their habbit their good manner etc. I'm affraid if I make something wrong that they didnt want me to do that—or can I just relax and do like what I always did? another question. Should I bring something for them when I come? Should I talk to their familiy as I stay there? I need to know more about american habbit, manners.

Finally, in the dialogue journal students can state complaints about the school, classroom activities, or actions and decisions of the teachers without disrupting the rest of the class, and the teacher can address those complaints in private. These two interactions come from a sixth grade student, Thuy, and a tenth grade student, Ravi.

> Thuy: Are you send the letter to Mrs. Nancy Reagan yet? Why everybody send us something we have to write a letter to them? Why too we don't have a P.E.?
>
> Teacher: If someone gives you something it is proper to say thank you. Because we cannot say thank you, we must write it. It is good manners.
>
> We didn't have P.E. today because of the assembly, but we'll have it tomorrow.

* * * * * *

> Ravi: I am sick and tired of school. I don't know why because they don't have a cooler in our school. It is always hot in this school. Sometimes I think of quitting the school. I think that the school is boring. Mrs. B why is it very hot in this school. I hate hot wether any way.
>
> Teacher: It can get hot in my room because we don't have any windows, and the air doesn't circulate well through the room. When the heat is on on a cold day or the air conditioning is on on a hot day, the room is all right. However, when the weather is good and no heat or air conditioning are needed in the school, these rooms get hot and stuffy.

If students are pulled from regular classes for ESL instruction, they may write in the journal to their ESL teacher about problems they are having in the regular classes. The regular classroom teacher may not realize that there are problems, because he or she is not used to teaching ESL students or because the students are not able or do not feel free to communicate openly in the regular classroom. With the student's permission, the ESL teacher can quickly remedy the problem by discussing it with the other teacher or by facilitating communication between that teacher and the student.

These are only a few examples of the types of problems that students might discuss in the privacy of the journal. All students are faced with troubling issues at some point. The journal gives them a place to try to work out their problems with someone else.

The Teacher Can Individualize Language and Content Learning

It doesn't really matter how proficient in writing students are. It is something they can all do and in which they can all achieve and experience some sort of success, whether they dictate their entries to the teacher or write long pieces independently.

Ruth Sedei, 1st and 2nd grade ESL teacher

I try to keep more or less a conversational tone. I try not to talk down to the students, and I try to stretch them a little bit. But I also want to find a level on which we can communicate. I will often rework my sentences to try to find a word that I think they'll understand. I do want them to understand.

Dawn Center, 1st and 2nd grade ESL teacher

In most classes with nonnative English speakers, students have a wide range of English proficiency levels. Students just beginning to learn English, oral or written, may be unable to keep up with the work others are doing and feel lost. But even those students can put something in a journal—a picture or a couple of words if nothing more—and receive a response, thus participating in the activities of the rest of the class. In responding, teachers can adjust their language so it is appropriate to each student, at a level that can be understood but is still challenging. The two interactions below were written on the same day in Leslee Reed's sixth grade class. The first one is with Kemmy, a Vietnamese student who had recently started school in the United States, had never attended school previously, had a very low level of English proficiency, and, at the time this entry was written, was doing little in class besides simple language exercises and writing in his journal. The second comes from Michael, a sixth grader from Burma, whose entry about Valentine's Day we read earlier, and who was making considerable progress in learning English.

Kemmy: today we are doing spelling is good and today I am so happy so funny . . . sompob He have New journal and He so happy and I have two journal I am have two . . . Andy He 3 journal.

Teacher: Andy has his 3rd journal. Sompob has his 4th journal and Kemmy has his 2nd journal. You all are writing in your journal every day.
Today we had a spelling bee. Kemmy spelled words for us. It was fun. I am glad Kemmy is spelling.

* * * * * *

Michael: I know I was saying the bad language. I will stop saying the bad language. I know why I get in trouble and I don't go out to play. I don't get in trouble. So I won't go out and play.

Today is friday the 13 and it is bad luck day because we got report card, math test and spelling test. How come people said friday 13 is the bad luck day?

Teacher: It is just an idea that people have! 13 is supposed to be a bad luck number and when it comes on Friday it is even more bad luck. Some people think Friday the thirteenth is good luck.

It is good for you to be out playing. It is very good for you to learn to control your temper and your tongue.

Kemmy uses simple vocabulary and syntax and repeats words and phrases he has learned so far. In response, the teacher uses simple sentences and words Kemmy knows and has used in his entry. She also refers to him by name rather than with "you" in the early stages of his writing, to catch his attention. His name was the one word he recognized immediately, and she hoped that upon seeing it he would want to read what she had written about him. (Later, when she knew he was reading and understanding her entries, she changed to "you".)

Vocabulary and syntax are considerably more advanced in Michael's journal, and he and the teacher discuss a cultural point and work through a problem he is having in school.

Because teachers can tailor their writing to the writing of each student, correct language forms and structures the student has attempted to used can be modeled in the context of genuine language use. In the example below the teacher uses and expands on many of the same phrases that Michael has used. The similar structures are italicized here to illustrate the point. They were not emphasized by the teacher.

Michael: Mrs. Reed today morning you said this is *my lovely friends* right? She told me about book story name is "the lady first in the air." She tells me *this lady* was first in the air, and she is flying the Pacific ocean, and she lose it everybody find her but *they can't find it. They loocked in the ocean still not here.* Did she know everything of book?

Teacher: *My lovely friend Mrs. P* reads a lot. She has read the book about *Amelia Earhart.* It is a good story and it is a true story. *They looked and looked but never found her airplane or her.*

This example clearly demonstrates language modeling. Of course, it would not be possible or desirable for the teacher to always directly model particular structures and vocabulary, for the interaction would quickly become stilted and unnatural. More often, modeling takes the form of correct English usage by the teacher, stated roughly at the student's level of ability, and related to something the student has written about. In the interaction below, for example, the teacher restates roughly what Andy has said about each topic but adds to it in each case, in a conversational style.

> Andy: today morning is picture I don't teacher is help me. thanks teacher.
> the present you picture. you is happy me is delighted. "thank teacher"
> today tree is flowerpot change good change
> and today is Miss V— vicariousness
> Miss P— come

> Teacher: Yes, I was happy to help you this morning with your work. The picture you made of me is very good. Thank you. I like it!
> You put your cutting into a flower pot because it has roots on it. It is ready to grow.
> Miss V— is sick. I hope she will come on Monday.
> Miss P— is a good friend. Did she help your reading group?

One aspect of language modeling is the building of students' vocabulary. In the exchange with Andy above, the teacher writes, "Miss V— is sick" in response to Andy's comment, "Miss V— vicariousness." (Andy frequently used his Korean-English dictionary when writing in his journal, occasionally with startling results.) She also could have written, "Miss V— is absent." In the interaction below with Michael, the teacher supplies a word in her response that Michael wants to use but doesn't know, and he then uses it in his next entry.

> Michael: Mrs. Reed where did you got the Chinese or Japan *counter*. I don't know the name so I did not write it.

> Teacher: The *abacus* is an old, old way of doing math. Chinese, Japanese and I would guess Burmese people have used that for an adding machine for hundreds of years.

> Michael: My grandfather know how to count with the *abacus*. He used for the *count the money*.

Teacher: The *abacus* is a fine way of calculating! It takes a little practice, but it is really good.
[Emphasis added.]

In an exchange with Jung An, a sixth grade student from Korea, the teacher builds on his vague reference to "math" by reviewing the specific concepts involved in the class's study of geometry.

Jung An: I like the math we did to day but I feel sorry for Mrs. G____
[the substitute teacher]

Teacher: Teaching math to 34 students with different abilities is tricky. Reviewing geometry and using it to make a design helped everyone to use metric measure, and to use radius, diameter, and concentric circles.

When the teacher uses vocabulary that the student doesn't understand, the words can be explained and clarified in later entries, as in this interaction with Claudia, a sixth grade student from El Salvador, whose writing about her hen appeared earlier.

Claudia: Maybe I will be bringing more tamales or pupusas so I will try to do it.

Teacher: You are so thoughtful! Jana and I appreciate the delicious tamales!

Claudia: *Why do you say that I am thoughtful? I can't understand what you mean by calling me thoughtful!*

Teacher: You are thoughtful! You bring goodies for me and Jana and you help us a lot! That is really great!

Claudia: Oh thank you for saying that what I do is great.
[Emphasis added.]

The potential for individualized learning is not confined to features of language use, but can involve course content and other topics as well. Journal discussions can allow further exploration of any topic the student is interested in. For example, U Chal, a student from Korea, asks the questions below which provide an opening for further discussion of the sixth grade class's lessons on maps and for repetition of key terms and concepts from these lessons.

U Chal: What is the good map for sailer?

Teacher: The mercator map is a good one for sailors.

U Chal: How do the boat now what diretion he go?

Teacher: The boat uses a compass to know the direction it is going. A long time ago the sailors on boats looked at the stars to tell directions.

U Chal: What map don't have distosan?

Teacher: The best map is the globe. It is too hard to carry—so the best flat map is the equal area map. It shows almost no distortion.

U Chal: If polar map is distoriation why is good for planes?

Teacher: The polar map has distortion on countries near the equator. For countries near the poles it is very true. You ask a fine question. You are thinking!

When Edwin, a 10th grade student from El Salvador, comments about Central America, the teacher's response extends considerably the information that he presents.

Edwin: Yesterday I watched a news about the Contras in Nicaragua. It was a very interesting news. It said that the only country who can stop that revolution in Nicaragua and in the other Central American countries is the United States. It said that the other countries such as El Salvador, Honduras are in war because of Nicaragua. It said if the United States would bring peace to Nicaragua all the other countries such as El Salvador and Honduras would be in peace too. In the news said the United States don't want more yonger to died.

Teacher: I was interested in your comments about the war in Nicaragua. I think the U.S. will become more and more involved in the civil wars in Central America, and we will be hated by some of the people of those countries for being there. Then, if we are very much involved, we will be hated by others if we try to leave. That is more or less what happened in Vietnam. On the other hand, Vietnam was the other side of the world, and Central America is right here in the Western Hemisphere and close to the Panama Canal, which is vital to the U.S. I truly don't know what we should do, but I see it as very difficult for us to bring peace to those countries. How can we avoid getting into the wars ourselves?

Edwin: I think that many countries get into wars just because of nothing, but other countries have enough reason to get into them. Many countries can avoid getting into the wars if they are more friendly and if they are peaceful countries. The United States is a friendly and peaceful country, but the United Sates always want to help other countries in anything she can and I think it is very nice of her. I guess what the United States want is to bring peace to all the countries in the World but that's impossible.

When the journals focus on the content of a course, rich discussions can occur that supplement and extend information discussed in class. For example, a team of fifth grade ESL and content area teachers in San Antonio has developed what they call *Think and Write Journals* in science and social studies (described in Kessler, 1989). Topics are not entirely open-ended, but rather finely tuned to units of study just completed. The format is also prescribed—a summary of the unit in the first paragraph, reflection on what part of the unit the writer liked best or would like to know more about in the second paragraph, and a statement about aspects of the topic that the writer does not understand in the third paragraph. Anita, a fifth grader from Mexico, and her teacher wrote the following:

Anita: I learned waht the Revolutan was about and how the cottin gin was working.
  The part I liked best was whene we had the revolutan and went free and had freedom and liverty even if I don't undersand it.
  I don't undersand why we brock from grait brente.

Teacher: The United States broke away from Great Britain so that we could be free and independent. We didn't want Great Britain to tell us what to do.[3]

Even though Anita's written English proficiency was limited, she was still able to reflect on her studies and express her puzzlement. The teacher's reply gave her not only an explanation, but also the spelling of Great Britain.

---

[3]Excerpted, with permission, from Kessler, 1989.

The way that a teacher's writing can be varied to push individual students' thinking in different ways is demonstrated clearly in the following group of teacher entries written on the same day by Leslee Reed to students in her sixth grade class. The class had read a story about an owl, and several students mentioned it in their journals. The focus of each teacher entry was different, responding to the focus of the different student entries and challenging each student's thinking at a different level.

To Fernando: The owl's picture and story were fun to see. Do you think the owl is wise?

To Claudia: I've heard people say, "He's as wise as an owl!" I wonder why people say that. Did you think this owl was wise?

To Benny: How do you think the author felt about the owl in that story? Did he write about the owl as though it had human or bird characteristics?

To Nicky: Which of the characteristics of the owl were anthropomorphic and which were avian? Do you think the owl did remember? Is that avian?

The Teacher Gains Information That Can Assist in Lesson Planning

I find that journal writing is sort of the kernel of my teaching. When I sit down to do journals, I am doing a kind of resume of my day, and of each child. As I'm writing each child, I'm mentally thinking about that child. I conjure up in my mind that child on that day. . . . Then as I'm reading his journal I'm seeing if what I sensed as a teacher came through to him as a student. Often it becomes clear then in my lesson plans, OK, this did not go over well. I'll need to get this over from a different point of view. So [the journal] becomes a planning tool, a core from which I'm planning not only tomorrow's work but, frequently, next week's work. For me, it makes my whole school year flow, because I have a constant finger on the pulse of the children.

Leslee Reed, 1988, pp. 70 & 71

Students' questions and interest in various topics expressed in the journals can provide input for planning future lessons. U Chal's questions about maps, shown earlier, and Michael's question, shown in the example below, showed the teacher how much they understood about the lesson, gave her a chance to re-explain it, and indicated what might need to be covered again with the rest of the class.

Michael: In the story of Yoko's grandmother I don't understand what mean the mouse is the most powerful being in the world?

Teacher: In our story the mouse was looking for the most powerful being to marry his daughter. He looked and looked. At last he learned that mice are powerful! They can do things that the sun, the clouds, the wind and the wall cannot do. Yoko's Grandmother told the story to show that we do not need to go looking for something more powerful. Each one of us has power. We need to use it.

The writing also gives the teacher information about students' language and writing abilities, a permanent, ongoing record of each student's progress in nonassigned writing that can be reviewed throughout the year. For example, contrast the following samples, excerpts from entries written early and late in the school year by Ruqayya, a fourth grade student who had recently arrived from Pakistan.

Ruqayya:
Sept. 3
I like to fly.
I like school.
I like to play.
I don't lik fish
I like this day.

May 19
today I was the all most the winner but I just miss the word. So the Sonia was the winner. I'm still very happy that she wan and in the aqua [reading] group their was too winner one was Rofina how was the winner and one was Nhung how was the winner.

During the year of writing Ruqayya moved from a list based on a familiar language pattern to more extended and complex discussion of a single topic. While the early simple sentences are grammatically more correct and the later entry has more errors, the later entry is much more advanced. The teacher can see how much progress Ruqayya has made, which structures she is attempting, which ones she uses correctly, which ones have not yet been acquired, and where she might concentrate her learning in the future.

Some teachers plan structure and vocabulary lessons around mistakes and interesting usages they find in students' journals. For example, if they see several students having the same problem with a particular word or structure, they might extract several examples from the journals (after asking students' permission and changing anything that might allow identification) for a class discussion or exercise. The danger with picking out and discussing errors is that students might get the idea that they shouldn't be making errors at all, and lose confidence and fluency in their writing. Whenever the form of students' journal writing becomes the focus of class discussion, students need to be reassured that this attention is not intended as criticism of their writing, nor do they need to worry about making such errors in the future. Their writing, in this case, is simply being used as data for class reflection on English language usage.

The information the teacher receives is not limited to understanding of course content or language development. As students share the customs of their country, the teacher's knowledge about them and their world is enriched, and they can be assured that the teacher considers their culture worthwhile. In the exchange below, Mario, a sixth grader from Mexico, explains a custom in his native state, Chihuahua, Mexico.

> Mario: you know why I like animals so much speallsh [especially] horses and dogs cause you know that thing you have on your soamck [stomach] when your bron they beeryed it on my grandfather ranch.
>
> Teacher: I knew you especially liked animals but I did not know that it was because your umbilical cord was buried on your grandfather's ranch. You're very lucky—that makes you feel close to your Grandfather and to Chihuahua!

Students Have the Opportunity to Use Writing for Genuine Communication

To achieve language flexibility pupils must apply whatever is studied to situations in which they have something to say, a deep desire to say it, and someone to whom they genuinely want to say it.

Walter Loban, 1986, p. 610

What I have learned from the journals is how to write about my ideas . . . I can write what I want, and when I am writing, I have ideas about what to write. I sometimes don't like it when teachers tell me what to write and I'm not interested in what I'm writing about. I feel bored and don't enjoy it. The best thing about the journal is it keeps you thinking about what you are writing.

12th grade ESL student

Despite the tremendous interest in the past several years in providing more opportunities for writing and in improving the writing of nonnative English speaking students, much in-school writing continues to be done in response to specific teacher assignments, about teacher-assigned topics, with no particular audience in mind, and for no purpose other than evaluation of the student's writing ability (Applebee, 1984). Interest in writing has brought with it the concern for writing assessment, and it is not uncommon for students in ESL classes to spend most of their writing time practicing for periodic tests in which they produce a writing sample for evaluation. The result is often canned, stilted writing, without personality or voice, that strives but fails to follow the models presented in class (Raimes, 1984).

The dialogue journal can be a completely open-ended writing experience, a time when students can write freely about anything they want to, in any way they want to; a time to use writing to think through an issue or problem, without being constrained by the need for perfect form. For some students, this might be their only nonstructured writing experience.

Not all teachers who use dialogue journals are particularly interested in their use to facilitate writing development, but those who are have reported encouraging results. Some have found that students whose writing on classroom assignments shows little promise express themselves much more clearly and eloquently in the journal. Compare, for example, the writing of two sixth graders, Ben, from the Philippines, and Simon, from Korea, on a typical kind of essay assignment at the end of a social studies unit—to compare and contrast the grasslands and desert—with parts of entries from their dialogue journals.

Ben's grasslands and desert essay, shown below, is somewhat dull and lifeless. He has fulfilled the assignment, pulling together his class notes on similarities and differences, but there isn't much else to it.

> The difference between the grassland is the grassland has water. And it also has grass. And it also has animals (like cows, chickens, dogs).
>   The difference between the grassland and the dessert is the people that lives in the dessert move from one place (that has water) to the other. The dessert has only have few waters. The desert has only a few people that live there.

In contrast, sometime during the class's study of the grasslands and desert the teacher brought in some animal bones, and Ben wrote the following in his journal (this is an excerpt from a longer entry that day):

The grasslands that we are doing is Europe. I found most of the information I wanted so far that I needed and the ones that you said to do. I got a chance to look at all those weird bones. They're weird because I usually see them with their skins, bones, and hair and *with* their eyes or eyeballs. Where did you get all of those bones? Did you got them from the desserts? I feel sorry for the turtles or the animals that lived in the deserts and got run over by those cruel men and women that runned over those sweet, nice, adorable animals. I like and loved tame animals.

There are grammatical imperfections in both pieces, but the same topic comes to life in the journal. Ben is engaged with the topic and able to relate it to his own experience, and he is writing to an audience he knows is interested in it as well.

Simon, a student with learning disabilities, produced a list of similarities and differences in his "essay," perhaps copied from his or some other student's notes.

differences

grassland has rain	desert land has no rain
many people	some people
it has water	it has no water
they has big city	they has no big city
has many anlmer [animals]	has little anlmer

similarities

it has land	it has land
it has people	it has people
they can go fishing	they can go fishing
has air port	has air port
[etc.]	

His dialogue journal writing had many weaknesses as well, but one day, after a bird he had been taking care of died, he wrote the following.

I like the bird. I give some food but he ded but It was 95 to grist [degrees] but I think he was cool. I barisd [buried] the bird and I put a sign abut [above] the bird. I had many bird at Korea but I like the bird but he ded but I like the bird best in my life and he was a baby and he can not fly and I did not know what to do. I can not sit on the bird the bird will be packaah (?). I have pauve I had the bird went I grel up [I pretended (?) I had the bird when I grew up]. I barad my sife [I buried it myself]. When I grow up I will relmader [remember] the bird. It was the best bird I had in my life and my frilme [family] like too.

Simon's description of his experience with the bird is repetitious and so full of spelling errors that it is indecipherable in places. He is also writing about a personal experience rather than an academic topic, which is probably easier for him. But in the journal he is showing that he can reflect on and write about events in his life. A teacher who had his assigned essay as the only example of his writing would have no way of knowing he had that ability.

As dialogue journal writing takes place over a period of time, it can become closely interrelated with other writing that students do in school, both influencing and being influenced by it. For example, the study of the grasslands and desert animals stimulated Ben's journal writing. A teacher might build on Simon's interest in and experience with birds to help him write a social studies essay focused on birds in the grasslands or desert.

An elementary ESL teacher observed that the relationship between journal writing and more formal academic writing is a natural one for her students:

> The students write in the journals in exquisite detail about things they do—field trips, family outings, school projects—and they want to use those pieces as the basis for writing they're doing in other classes. They come to me and say, "Can I copy this to use in class?" They've already done some thinking about the event, have already processed it in writing in their journal, and that's what they want to work with.
>
> Dawn Center, 1st and 2nd grade ESL teacher

High school teachers have also found that when students must produce samples of their writing for evaluation by the school or county, some like to work through the topic or a related one in their journal first, as preparation for the evaluated writing.

Likewise, as students learn more about writing processes and conventions in other activities and assignments, they begin to apply this knowledge to their dialogue journal writing—paying closer attention to paragraphing, punctuation, grammatical form, and the like. Teachers using dialogue journals for extended periods of time (at least one semester) almost without exception report that they see improvements in the form of this writing.

Dialogue journals as a writing activity for students are not personal journals or journal logs in which students write day after day without receiving a response. The teacher is also writing, giving students an ongoing model of the writing of a more competent writer; not only on the level of words, phrases, and sentences, but also of thought processes, organization of thoughts, and overall fluidity and coherence of expression.

Teachers experienced with dialogue journals are convinced that they promote students' writing development. Quotations from some of these teachers provide a fitting conclusion to this section.

I saw students who really felt like they had nothing to say become quite good writers: They were not able to express themselves well before writing in the journal simply because they'd never tried it before, never before had the opportunity to communicate through writing.

> Ruth Sedei, 1st and 2nd grade ESL teacher

When students write about experiences they've had, they begin to realize that sentences and paragraphs can be expanded to portray the action, sights, sounds, and smells involved. Their entries get longer, more detailed, more lively because of the freedom they have to write ... I think the students who at first didn't like to write have benefited from it the most, because they have begun to like writing. They have become participants.

> Dawn Center, 1st and 2nd grade ESL teacher

The dialogue journal makes writing an everyday kind of experience. It's not just a thing that you do when you have a test or when you need to write a report or something, it can be a part of your everyday life. You can write about problems, hopes, desires, create a story, whatever. There's nothing to be afraid of. I don't want my students to be afraid, I want them to feel comfortable with writing and feel they can express thoughts on paper, and I think the journal has influenced their attitudes. They don't seem to be afraid of writing now. It is not a threatening type of thing to them anymore.

> Kelly Miller, 4th–6th grade ESL teacher

Writing and responding in dialogue journals has definitely improved my students' writing. They let down their guard and stop worrying about their writing. They have paragraph tests to take, and it's the hardest part of their curriculum. They know that mine is a writing class, priming them to pass that paragraph test. If they don't pass it, they don't move up to the next class. The dialogue journal is a way to improve their writing without all that pressure. They just write to me about what's going on with them.

> Normandy Lee, 9th–11th grade ESL teacher

There are only three times in the entire week that my students can write, just for the pleasure of writing [her students write in their dialogue journals three days a week]. It is not corrected or evaluated. It is a time for them to write to me, for me to enjoy reading what they have to say, and for me to respond to them. My goal is that they will understand that their words can command my attention, that they can get across feelings, can be poetic, can get something off their chest. I want them to believe that they can communicate by writing in English, that somebody thinks their writing is neat and understands what they wrote, no matter how convoluted it was.

And finally, I want them to see that they can understand what I write to them.

Juanita Zientara, 9th and 10th grade ESL teacher

Students Have an Additional Opportunity for Reading

Two basic necessities for learning to read are the availability of interesting material that makes sense to the learner and an understanding and more experienced reader as a guide.

Frank Smith, 1985, p. 7

The best part of the journal is reading . . . no, writing . . . no, reading . . . well, both.

4th grade ESL student

Every Monday the kids come in and the journals are there and they want to read.

Dawn Center, 1st and 2nd grade ESL teacher

An important part of dialogue journal writing is the reading that occurs as a part of the interaction. Every time the teacher writes, a reading text is produced for student consumption—a text that is usually closely tied to the student's life experience and to what the student has just written, that incorporates and expands on some of the concepts, words, and structures the student has expressed, and introduces new ones. With beginning readers this opportunity can be a panacea. It is difficult to find reading texts for beginning readers that are interesting as well as manageable and don't require a lot of background information and concepts supplied by the teacher.

Reading can begin as soon as the student has put something in the journal, even if it is a picture or one or two words. The teacher can write a few words or a simple sentence in response, read it to the student, and then ask the student to read it alone. Thus, one of the student's first experiences with reading takes place in the context of genuine communication.

With more advanced readers, the benefit may relate more to the motivation to read that the teacher's writing generates. Even among those students who are reluctant to write in their journals or read other class materials, there are few who are not eager to read what the teacher has written to them.

Teachers report feeling the same compelling motivation to read what their students have said to them. One teacher, who always dreaded reading and correcting student papers, described driving home from school and reading the journals opened on the seat next to her.

Some Words of Caution

We close this section about benefits with some words of caution. First, the last two benefits discussed have to do with the development of reading and writing abilities. There is no hard, empirical evidence that writing in dialogue journals actually does cause improvement in students' reading and writing relative to other kinds of activities that students could engage in. Such a study would be very difficult to do because of the many variables involved. What we have presented here are testimonials by teachers and students, our own experiences with and observations of journal use in the classroom, and studies of the journal texts that were produced. These strongly point to the positive effects that dialogue journals can have on reading and writing.

Second, the benefits cited here seem to occur when the journals are not used for the primary purpose of improving reading and writing abilities, but for the purpose of promoting communication between students and teachers. Because of recent increased interest in schools in the development of specific skills, we cannot emphasize this point enough. There are many opportunities in the classroom, outside of dialogue journal writing, to work on developing various academic skills. When the journal is used for that purpose, it quickly becomes just another classroom exercise. The benefits discussed here are a result of the journal's being used as a way to communicate.

Finally, dialogue journal writing is not meant to substitute for an entire writing program, which must be much broader in scope. (See Jones, 1988, for a thorough discussion of this point.) There are important aspects of good writing that do not often occur in the journals. First, students do not often revise their writing content or style, a step that is crucial to producing a good piece of writing. Second, they do not receive direct feedback about its correctness or edit it, so there may be grammar, spelling, and punctuation errors that would be corrected in a more finished piece. Finally, the journals do not include all of the types of writing that students need to be able to do, including formal business letters, persuasive essays, and research reports.

Instead, dialogue journals need to be considered part of a complete program that includes all aspects of the writing process—brainstorming, drafting, composing, revising, editing, and publishing—as well as a variety of writing genres and styles (Jones, 1988).

CHAPTER 4

Using Dialogue Journals with Different Kinds of Students

"When we give [people] the time, materials, and encouragement to write, they use whatever they *do* know in amazing ways."

Lucy Calkins, 1986, p. 37

One of the most compelling features of dialogue journals is their adaptability for use in different situations and with different kinds of students. Leslee Reed first used them with sixth graders who were native English speakers (Staton et al., 1988), and later with students from other countries learning English (Kreeft et al., 1984). When she and researchers studying her practice began to talk about dialogue journals and show examples of the students' writing, teachers across the country and overseas immediately saw the contribution that journals could make in their own classrooms and started using them with their students. Dialogue journals are now being used in a wide variety of educational settings.

In university courses, students interact with professors about a wide range of topics depending on the nature of the course—including concepts covered in the course, literature being read, writing in progress, adjustment to a new culture, and career goals (Steffensen, 1986, 1987, 1988; chapters in Peyton, 1990a). In these dialogues, students have consistent opportunities to use English in a variety of ways and to use and further develop higher levels of thinking and self-expression.

Writing with professors allows prospective and practicing teachers in teacher training courses and in in-service workshops to reflect on course content, their experiences in the classroom, and their development as teachers, and prepares them for keeping journals with their own students (Brinton & Holten, 1989; Roderick, 1986; Roderick & Berman, 1984; see also articles in *Dialogue*, September, 1988).

In adult basic education and literacy classes, adults at the beginning stages of learning English, or native English speakers who are nonliterate, can move beyond practicing discrete skills and slowly begin to experience written English as a means of personal empowerment, as they learn to discuss issues that are important to them (Auerbach & McGrail, in press; Hester, 1986; Klos, 1988).

Children at lower elementary levels in ESL and bilingual classrooms sometimes begin the dialogue journal by drawing or writing a few words, and gradually gain more facility as they continue to write and read the teacher's responses (Bailes, Searls, Slobodzian, & Staton, 1986; Flores & García, 1984; Peyton, 1990b; see also articles in *Dialogue*, April 1989). For migrant children, who may have had interrupted school experiences, dialogue journals can provide a highly social, nonthreatening way to lead them into other kinds of school-related reading and writing activities (Davis, 1983; Hayes & Bahruth, 1985; Hayes, Bahruth, & Kessler, 1986).

For foreign language students (Martin, 1989; Pesola & Curtain, 1989; Popkin, 1985), as well as for deaf children and adults, for whom English is often a second or foreign language (Bailes et al. 1986; Staton, 1985; Walworth, 1985, 1989; articles in *Dialogue*, December, 1987) the dialogue journal provides the opportunity to extend the use of English or the foreign language in an authentic, communicative way.

Dialogue journals are also used with mentally handicapped and learning disabled adults (Farley, 1986; Flores, Rueda, & Porter, 1986; Peyton & Steinberg, 1985). For some, who previously had been considered nonreaders and -writers, the dialogue journal becomes their first and most extended reading and writing experience.

Teachers and counselors of high risk students, who are not necessarily language limited but who have demonstrated little success in school, have found that these students can be motivated to read and write in a dialogue journal. The safety and distance of written interaction can open up communication possibilities that are blocked in oral, face-to-face conversations (McGuire, 1986; Staton, 1987).

In short, dialogue journals have proven flexible and adaptable to a wide variety of communication settings, and teachers continue to report success with them in situations that broaden the range still further. In this section we explain some ways that they can be used with different levels of students learning English.

Beginning Writers

My own view is that every child who can talk has the capacity to learn to write and also to seize the possibilities of written language with enthusiasm.

Frank Smith, 1983, p. 81

I think that all students benefit, but those at beginning levels benefit a lot. They have to start producing, they can't just sit back and do nothing, and it's a non-threatening way to get started. They just start out trying their wings, and I'm always amazed at what they can do.

Ruth Sedei, 1st and 2nd grade ESL teacher

With young children who are just learning to read and write in English or with adults who are nonliterate, either in their native language or in English, dialogue journal writing can be introduced whenever the student feels comfortable in the classroom and has developed some oral language facility. It can start out as an interactive picture book, in which student and teacher draw pictures for each other. As the student begins to learn to write letters and words, the teacher can label the pictures or write brief descriptions or explanations below them. Very quickly the student learns that marks on paper can convey a message to another person.

Ruth Sedei, for example, started using dialogue journals with her first and second grade students, all of whom were nonnative English speakers beginning to write in English and some of whom were nonliterate in their native languages, about a month after school began. They had adjusted to the routines of school life and had developed some oral language facility and some knowledge of words and letters. For one week she modeled the process of writing each day by thinking aloud about what she might write that day, exploring and deciding on some topics, and writing on a large sheet of butcher paper as the students watched. Then she discussed with them her process and what she had written. The next week, students wrote and drew on large sheets of looseleaf paper, and the class discussed what individual students had done. The third week the students received their own dialogue journal notebooks.

Mrs. Sedei's students spend the first 15 minutes of each day writing and drawing in their journals, while she takes care of such details as collecting lunch money. When they are finished, they place their journals in a box labeled "Journals" in a corner of the room. Later in the morning, during individual reading and writing time, those who wish to can continue writing in their journals before going on to their other writing work. Mrs. Sedei and an aide, working separately, take the journals from the box and spend about 20 minutes calling students over one by one for the students to talk about what they have drawn and written and to read their entries aloud. With students who have little to say about their entries or cannot remember what they wrote, questions and comments help them to remember, talk about, and extend their entries orally and to understand that whatever they wrote or drew is informative and valuable. Mrs. Sedei writes a reply immediately, writing slowly and reading aloud as she writes, and then she and the student read the reply together and sometimes discuss both its content and form. Students who want to write their entries rather than draw but are not yet able to do so alone can dictate them to Mrs. Sedei, the aide, or a peer tutor, who writes them as the student's entry, responds in writing, and helps the student read both the entry and the response.

The following examples give an idea of what beginning writers can do. (See also Peyton, 1990b, for a more detailed description of Ruth Sedei's approach with beginning writers and examples of young children's dialogue journal writing. For a profile of the development over time of a beginning writer see the profile of Catalina, a first grader from Colombia, in Chapter 8.) Figure 4 shows one of Catalina's early entries. She began by drawing pictures and asking for help to write the words she wanted. In her responses, the teacher tried to use some of those words. In Figure 5, José, a third grader from Belize, drew a school and labeled it with words he was learning. The teacher entered into the activity by labeling some of the picture herself (*kid* and *teacher*), and used some of José's words in her one-sentence response.

Figure 6a & b show a more extended interaction between Michelle, an eight-year-old deaf girl, and her teacher, who is also deaf. Michelle drew two "banana people," with a baby in the stomach of the woman, and the teacher commented on the baby. Michelle's responding picture shows that she understood what the teacher wrote. She also did some writing of her own, picking up on the word "baby."

Katie (Figure 7a & b), another deaf child, was doing much more writing than Michelle, but she made use of all means available to communicate—words, pictures, signs. If there was a word she didn't know how to write, she drew a picture of it (a hedge trimmer), or the Sign Language sign for it (the joined hands for "again"; the sign of the cross for "hospital"), or she spelled it as best she could ("side" for "said"). In her responses, the teacher included some of the words for things that Katie had drawn, modeling for her the language she needed, and also building on Katie's topic so she could read and write

Figure 4

October 2

play

read

eat

Do you read books at your house? What books do you like to read?

Figure 5

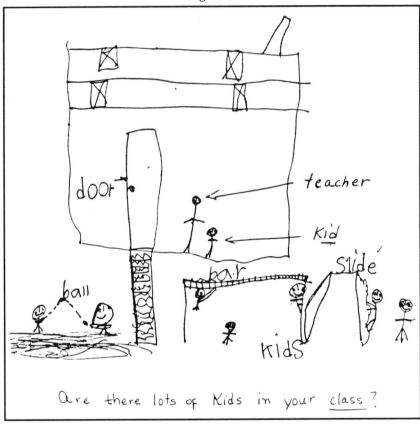

more about it. The result is an extended discussion about Katie's trip to the hospital.[4]

Although these two children are deaf, they can also be considered nonnative English speakers, since their first language is some form of Sign Language and written English is essentially a second language for them.

However the written interaction is begun in the early stages, students quickly realize that whatever they can say or sign can also be written. They see that their writing communicates something to someone else who wants to read it and who will always respond. What they read in that response is closely tied to their own writing efforts.

As students begin to become more aware of print, their journal entries

---

[4]Both examples are reprinted, with permission, from Bailes et. al., 1986.

Figure 6a

are often based on print they see around them in the classroom. The blackboard, posters, and books become a valuable resource for writing. One first grade ESL student, for example, labeled her picture with the names of fellow classmates, copied from their desks (Figure 8). Another copied the first part of the name of Christian, another student, for his entry about Christmas (Figure 9).

Phimporn, a 12-year-old from Laos, was placed in a sixth grade class because of her age, but she had had no schooling before starting school in the United States, was nonliterate in Lao, and had practically no oral English facility. As soon as she learned a little oral English, she started writing in a dialogue journal. The journal writing was a comfort to her, because it was a place where she could write and read like the other students in class. Her first entries consisted of structures she was practicing orally. When she exhausted those

Figure 6b

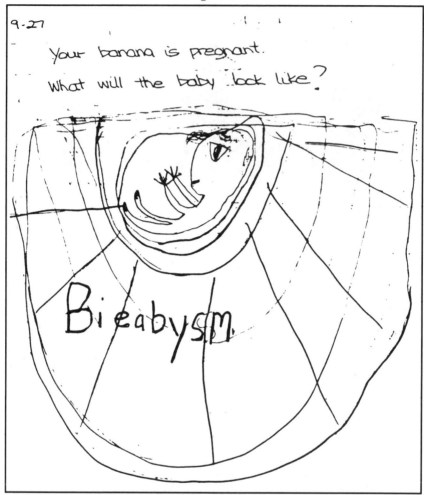

structures, she copied whatever she saw on the chalkboard or on charts in the room (Figure 10a, November).

As students continue to write in their journals over time, they accumulate an ongoing record of their own words and of messages written to them, which can become a reference that is always available for their further writing. They gradually move away from their dependence on environmental print and begin to sound out words and use invented spelling. In Figure 11, for example, Catalina, whose earlier entry was shown in Figure 4, writes, "I am happy with my crayons and my pencil. Today I am using my pencil and my crayons."

Students also move from writing only about objects in their imme-

Figure 7a

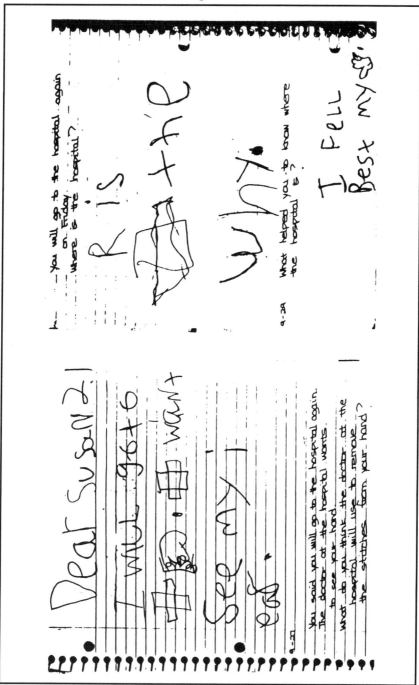

Figure 7b

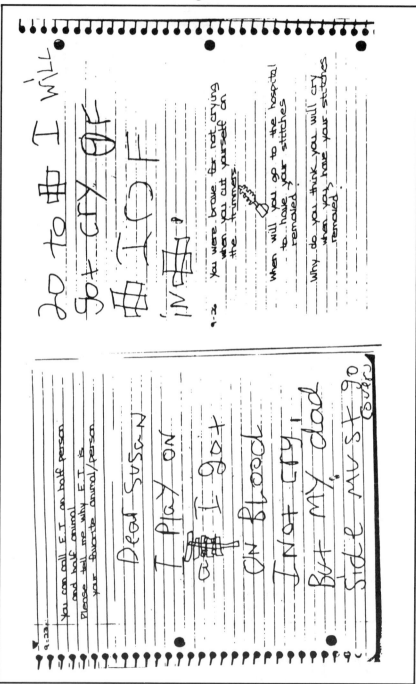

44

Figure 8

diate environment to writing about activities as well—initially, activities occurring in the present and, gradually, past and future ones. They also begin to show evidence that they are reading the teacher's writing and writing to the teacher as audience. This kind of development is shown in Figure 10b in Phimporn's June entry. She has moved from memorized structures and copying to writing about thoughts

Figure 9

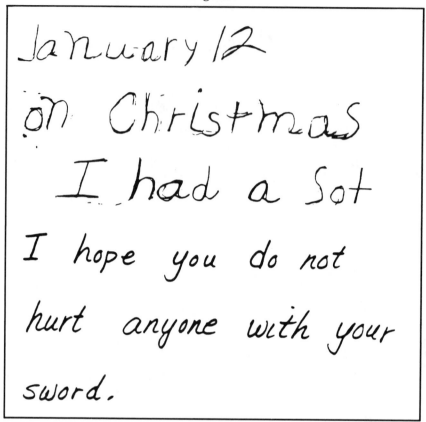

> January 12
> on Christmas
>   I had a Sot
> I hope you do not
> hurt anyone with your
> sword.

and events, and she is asking and answering questions with the teacher.

Literate Writers

Human beings have a deep desire to represent their experience through writing.

Lucy Calkins, 1986, p. 3

Students who are literate in their native language and more advanced educationally can begin to write independently in their journal very early. Keum, a sixth grader from Korea, knew very little English when he started school in the United States, but he did know how to write in Korean. Early in the year he frequently used his

Figure 10a—November

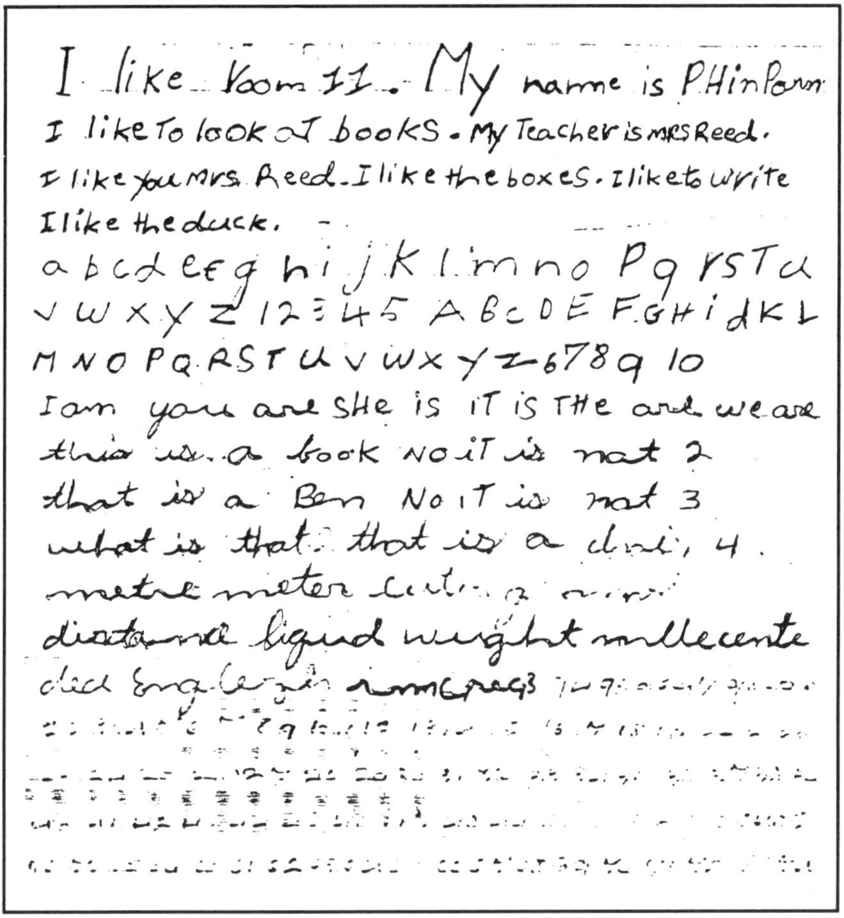

Korean-English dictionary to write his entries and to read the teacher's entries, as shown in Figure 12.

If the teacher or a bilingual classroom aide knows the student's native language, the dialogue can begin in that language rather than in English. After a few weeks some English words can be included— names of foods, school items, or other English vocabulary the student has been exposed to. As time progresses and more and more English words are included, the student may begin writing some English words as well, and the transition to English is made gradually, as the student seems ready. This assumes, of course, that the goal *is* for the student to learn English. If that is not the goal, then the dialogue can continue in the native language.

David, a fifth grader from Bolivia, for example, began the year

Figure 10b—June

Today PHimporn write to mrs R.
I am hot. Are you hot?
Today I read a book . Today I plap
hopskoch .

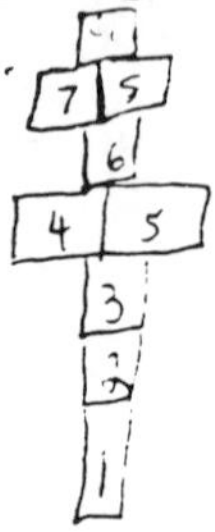

I went to mr L   classfo read .
I like mr L   s class, I like to go to
mr L   's class for Reading .
        You are learning to read better
everyday. You are talking and you
are reading and writing all in
English. You are learning.

writing in Spanish (October entry below) and the classroom aide responded in Spanish. As David's English vocabulary increased, he began to insert English words into his entries (November). By March, he and the teacher were writing consistently in English. There is some evidence of the influence of Spanish on his spelling ("jav" for "have," "liro" for "little," and "besbol" for "baseball") and word order ("the childre liro" for "the little children"), but many of the nonstandard features of his early writing (incorrect separation of words, incorrect use of capital letters, and lack of punctuation) have cleared up.

October

David: Nosotros fimos con mi hemano al parque a jugar con bisicleta des pues volvimos nosotros amicasa y salimo Hase compras al a hacer despues volvimos a mi casa y luego dormimos ala a manecer me levant y fuia laescuela.
[Translation: we went to the park with my brother to play on our bikes. After we came back home, we went

Figure 11

March 23

I am ape Waf
am Crayons an am
psow today I am
yousn am psow
an am Crayons

I am happy with your
writing. I can't believe it.
You can write many, many
words.
   Please don't lose your crayons.
Do you have a box to put them
in?

out shopping and later returned home. We went to sleep.
In the morning I got up and went to school.]

Teacher: Ahora me gustaría saber qué compraron cuando fueron
a hacer compras y a qué centro comercial fueron. Por
ejemplo, a mí me gusta el centro comercial de Seven
Corners porque es más pequeño, y encuentro casi siem-
pre todo lo que quiero.
   [Translation: Now I would like to know what you
bought when you went shopping, and which shopping
center you went to. For example, I like Seven Corners

Figure 12

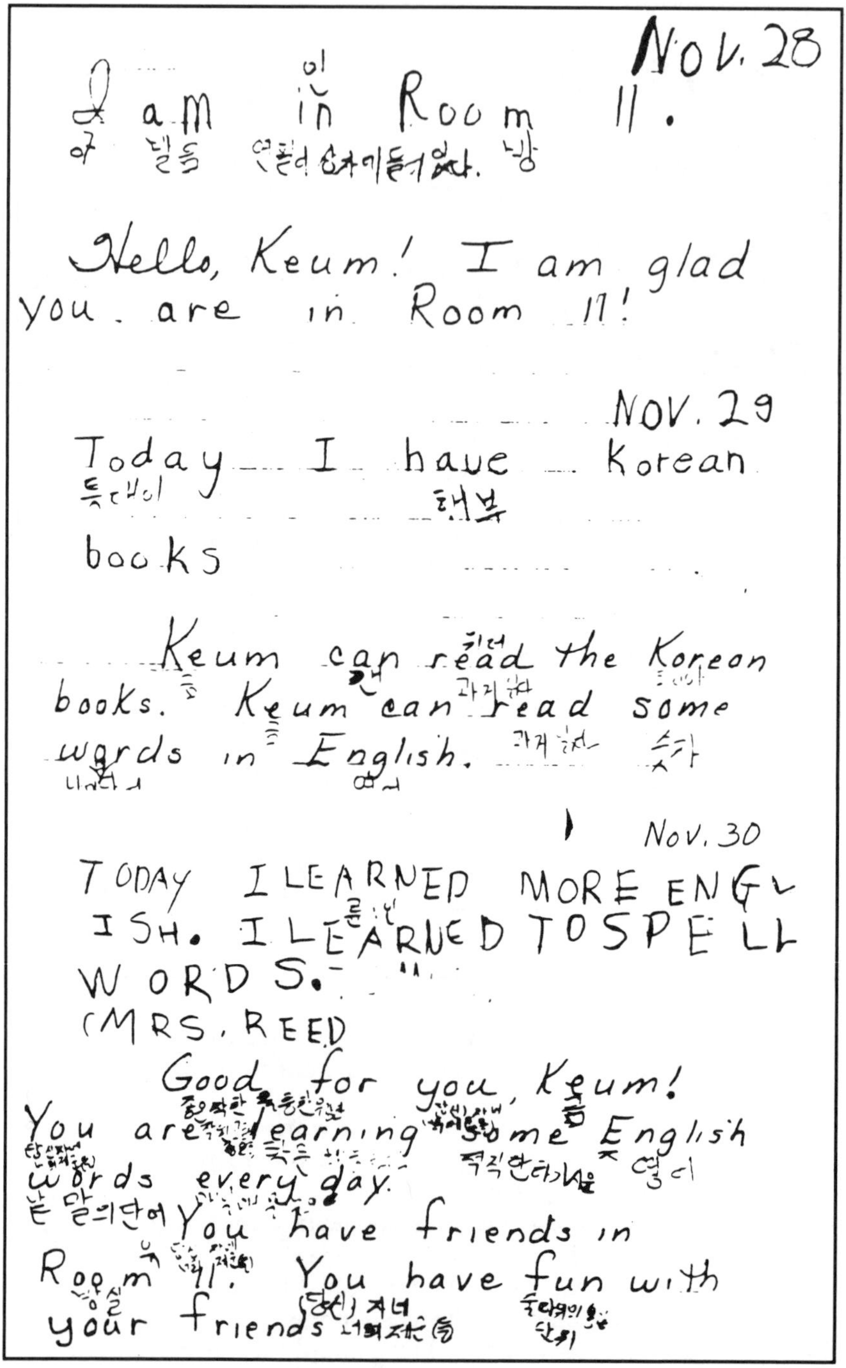

NOV. 28

I am in Room 11.
우 빌을 연더 호기에들어있나. 방

Hello, Keum! I am glad you are in Room 11!

NOV. 29

Today I have Korean
듯대이   책부
books

Keum can read the Korean books. Keum can read some words in English.
비대니   에

NOV. 30

TODAY I LEARNED MORE ENGLISH. I LEARNED TO SPELL WORDS.
(MRS. REED

Good for you, Keum! You are learning some English words every day. You have friends in Room 11. You have fun with your friends

50

shopping center, because it is smaller, and I can almost always find everything I want.]

November

David: Yo cuando llege a este pais no sabia el in gles, fumos con miermano alas clases de verano luego termino las clases nos fumos a nuestra casa . . . en la prueba yo mispell box no tengo mas que decirlo.

[Translation: When I came to this country, I didn't know English. I went with my brother to summer school. When I finished classes, we went home . . . on the test I misspelled "box." I don't have anything else to say.]

March

David: yes in Bolivia have 2 dog and jav a big animals and liro animals, and snake and a condor. and the miro the park and the parck have the childre liro play and jav soccer and besbol.

Teacher: I think your park is very, very big. Does your zoo in Bolivia have pandas? I wish our big pandas would have a little baby panda someday.

A profile of the year-long development of another student, Miguel, who also began writing in Spanish, is presented in Chapter 8.

More Advanced Writers

I think the more advanced students really benefit from the dialogue journal because they can ask questions about things. If we are studying some content area, we can just take off from where we stopped in class and explore it together.

Kelly Miller, 4th–6th grade ESL teacher

With students who are more proficient in written English, the journal is an excellent place for discussing topics being studied in class, current events, or personal concerns. It is also an opportunity for developing a more equal relationship between student and teacher, with the roles of teacher and student temporarily suspended, while they become collaborators in a discussion. One example of such collaboration comes from U Chal, a sixth grader from Korea, whose discussion of maps was shown in Chapter 3. U Chal was an extremely motivated student and loved to discuss what he was learning in science and geography classes.

U Chal: I am doing the report about White sharks and when I
          finish I am going to do about Dolphins if I have time.
          In Brazil they only use Celsius they have Fahrenheit
          but they use Celsius to see the temperature to cook and
          the doctors use only Celsius to see the body temperature.

Teacher: You know Celsius better than Fahrenheit temperatures
          then, don't you? We are going to be doing some thermom-
          eter reading here in the room. We'll use both scales.
          Dolphins or porpoises are unique animals. They seem
          to have a language.

U Chal: I never read about Fahrenheit until I come to the U.S.,
          the first time I come I saw a film of doctor and they find
          that one monkey had a fever and when he got the fever
          his body temperature was 115 F but I thoughth they
          was talking about 115 C but now I know the different of
          Celsius and Fahrenheit.
          I know and I read that scientist was stunding about
          dolphins language. Last year when I was in Brazil I was
          in the beach and I saw a dolphin dead on the sand and
          when I touch the skin is like sofet and then when I eat
          the lunch and I go to see the dolphin some birds was
          eating the dolphin.

Teacher: The dolphins have even been trained to do undersea work
          for the Navy. They seem to have an intelligence. The
          birds help to clean the beach by eating the dead animals.
          The dolphin's skin has no scales—we expect an animal
          that looks like a fish to have scales.

Another student, a sixth grader from the Philippines, loved to discuss events that were prominent in the news at the time— popular
music groups, the Academy awards, the Presidential election, space
initiatives. In the interaction that follows he and the teacher begin
writing about a "Nemesis" meteorite which may have struck earth in
prehistoric times, possibly causing a dramatic drop in temperature
and the extinction of the dinosaurs. They then move on to discuss the
things that scientists are learning from space exploration.

Ben: . . . That five days vacations was fast! It seems like yester-
          day we had the first day off of the five days vacation. It
          feels like a fire ball passing.
          Speaking of fire balls. Did you listened to the news

about a meteor about Earth's size might collide with Earth? They might have figured out about the dinosaurs.

They think that a meteor might have clided with Earth a long, long time ago during the dinosaurs time. They think that's going to happen again. But they already know what to do. There going to send a remote control rocket right into the meteor so it wouldn't collide with earth. They I think there going to send the powerful rocket in the whole wide countries or world.

Teacher: Yes, I heard about the meteor theory being a good way of explaining what happened to all of the dinosaurs. I'm not worried about getting hit with another meteor!

Ben: I know. There's nothing to worry about. They will think of using rocket. There's a lot of way to destroy those meteor that comes near and skid near Earth. I wonder how many planets did they explored beside Venus and that planet that has a ring Saturn. It was amazing when they discovered that Venus has a ring just like Saturn. Our Scientist today is getting better and better all the time. Pretty soon there going to be all famous and explore planets that never had been explored before in life . . .

Teacher: . . . Some of our scientists will become famous because they are learning more and more about space. Saturn has 52 rings—not just one. They've also discovered that some of the rings are braided like a chain!

Ben: An it also has two moons traveling at the same time around Saturn. Isn't that right? But there's more than two moons that I now. It's really, really amazing how they discover things like that with modern machines and all. Another planet has a ring too! I forgot what was the name but I know there's one more planet that has ring. What was that name of that planet again, Mrs. Reed? I think the planet is Venus. But I'm not sure. Imagine that. All the time those rings has been around Venus for many, many thousands of years and no one noticed it until 1979 . . .

Teacher: We need a new reference book on astronomy so we can see which planets have the rings and the moons. All of our old books don't have all of the new information, do they?[5]

[5]Reprinted, with permission, from Staton, 1989.

In each of the discussions above, the teacher has discovered what the student knows, and has expanded on and advanced the student's thinking about the topic by offering new information and reactions.

When the teacher asks questions along with making comments, students are pushed to think further about what they have written, as in the following two examples from Sonia, a sixth grader from Mexico, and Jung An, a sixth grader from Korea.

Sonia: We also saw a bunch of bats. They were very ugly. We swam in the Virgin River but it was rushing to much. When we came back we saw a yellow line dividing the sky in half. We saw blue sky and yellow sky.

Teacher: The yellow sky was over the city, wasn't it? What does that tell you about the air?

I've never been in the Virgin River. Is it large? Did you swim in the Colorado River? I did—and do you know what happens when you swim in that river?

Sonia: Yes, the yellow was over the sky. The yellow stuff tells me that people smog up the air. The Virgin River is relly big. In some places its muddy but were we were camping it was clear. It was like a rushing river. I didn't go swimming in the Colorado River. What happens if you swim in the Colorado River?

Teacher: When you swim in the Colorado River you have to take a shower afterward because your body is covered with silt. (Silt is fine pieces of dirt!) It is really strange because the silt is red colored . . .

* * * * * *

Jung An: A poem
Eagles are graceful birds
They attack lamb out of herds
They protect their young with their lives
As well as mate for lives
when attacked it
will fight back
I just love eagles

Teacher: Your poem shows a lot of knowledge about eagles! Have you ever marveled at their ability to soar and climb?

Jung An: Yes but unlike falcons eagles has muscles for climbing and soaring instead of flapping.

The various levels of writing illustrated in this section obviously do not represent a full range of student abilities. Interactions with adults, for example, both in and out of the university, would look much different (cf. Jones, 1988; Peyton, 1990a, for examples of adult ESL students' dialogue journal writing). But this discussion of writing with students from very beginning to more advanced levels should illustrate that the journal interaction can take whatever form it needs to take, depending on the goals of the teachers and the needs and interests of the students involved.

CHAPTER 5

GETTING STARTED

I start establishing the journal routine with my students immediately.

Leslee Reed, 1988, p. 57

Getting started with dialogue journals is quite simple, but before starting, it is a good idea to think about a few management issues such as:

- what students will write in;
- with which students you will write;
- how often the students will write and how often you will respond;
- when the writing will take place;
- how much the students will write;
- and how you will introduce the idea of dialogue journals.

Each of these issues is discussed in turn, focusing on students who are already literate, have had experience with reading and writing, and are working independently. Some ways for getting started with young children or other beginning writers are outlined in Chapter 4.

What to Write in

Each student should have a bound, portable notebook, used only for this purpose, rather than sheets of looseleaf paper passed back and forth. (As discussed earlier, computer disks or electronic mail message systems can be used instead of notebooks.) The notebook allows an ongoing dialogue that is kept in one place and can be referred to at any time during the year. Students can either choose their own notebooks or they can all be given the same kind of notebook by the teacher. In either case, the notebooks should be large enough to allow extended exchanges, yet small enough to be easily carried by the teacher. The advantage of having the same notebook for everyone is simply that it makes the stack of journals easier for the teacher to manage and transport. Some teachers prefer spiral bound notebooks, although some complain that they get tangled easily and students are more likely to tear out pages for other purposes; others like composition books; some even use blue exam books; some have students make their own notebooks and design the covers. With young writers, notebooks with primary lines can be purchased or made. An advantage of having blank covers, either on self-made or purchased notebooks, is that students can decorate them. Students may fill several notebooks during the school year.

A place should be established where the notebooks (if used) will be left after students have written in them and picked up by the students after the teacher has written.

With Whom to Write

Most teachers who enjoy dialogue journals would like to use this practice with all of their students. Although time constraints and large numbers of students may make this impossible, there are different ways that the journals can be managed. If a teacher has several classes each day, one or two can be chosen to keep dialogue journals. Another option is to have classes write on alternate days, to stagger the teacher's responding time. Another might be to give some students a choice about writing. In short, it is not necessary to keep dialogue journals with all students at all times.

How Often to Write

The frequency of the writing depends on how often the class meets, how many students the teacher is writing with, the course objectives, how much class time is devoted to the students' writing, and how much time the teacher is able to spend writing in the journals. The writing needs to occur regularly and continually. A daily exchange of the journal is ideal for creating a true sense of dialogue and maintaining a continual interchange of ideas. But many teachers find that, for various reasons, they cannot or do not want to maintain this schedule. Most agree that two or three times a week is necessary to maintain the dialogue and that the teacher should write regularly, if not each time the students write. If too much time elapses between entries the writing tends to lose its interactive quality, and it becomes more like a letter or even a series of short compositions.

Whatever schedule is decided on, it needs to be maintained so that the writing becomes almost a routine. Most teachers have said that they believe one reason their use of dialogue journals has been successful is that students understand the schedule and so can anticipate when they will be writing and when they will receive a reply.

When to Write

Most teachers give their students time to write during school hours. In self-contained classes where students spend considerable time during the day, they may be given some time when they first arrive to read the teacher's entry and begin to write their own, and then keep their journals with them to write when they have time during the day or when they think of something to say. In classes where considerable free time is given for individual student reading and writing, the students may decide where the dialogue journal will fit into their other writing activities.

When students spend limited time each day in the class (such as an hour-long class period), dialogue journal time can be scheduled at the beginning of class as a warm-up or at the end as a wind-down. If the class session includes a break, scheduling the writing before the break allows those students who desire extra time to write to do so during the break.

Teachers usually respond outside of class time. But if students are in the classroom for the entire day and have free reading/writing time, the teacher may spend that time responding to journals as they are completed. This gives students the chance to view the teacher as a writer too.

How Much to Write

It may be desirable to set a minimum amount that students must write each time (three lines or sentences, for example), at least in the beginning. Beyond that, the amount of writing done should be left to the individual student. Students should understand that long, polished pieces are not required. Most teachers roughly match their students' writing for length.

Introducing the Idea

It is a good idea to begin using dialogue journals as early in the year as possible, so they quickly become part of the regular classroom routine. If students already know some English, the journals can be started right away. If they are beginning English learners who are expected to write in English, it is best to wait about a month until they have acquired some minimal English vocabulary.

When introducing the idea, the teacher can explain to students that they will be having a continuing, private conversation in writing. It is important to stress that dialogue journals provide a way to communicate with each other rather than presenting them as a way to learn language or writing. In the journals, the students can write about whatever they want unless there is a specified focus for the writing, such as course content. (See the discussion in Chapter 2.) They can get information or give their opinions about class activities and assignments, write about their interests, problems, or concerns, ask for help or more information, even complain about things that are bothering them. They will not receive a grade, and their writing will not be corrected. Instead, they will receive a regular response from the teacher. Some teachers hand out a sheet of paper on which they explain the idea, give some general guidelines, and suggest possible directions the dialogue might take.

Most teachers have found that journal writing is most productive when it becomes routine, in the positive sense—students know when they will be writing and when they will receive a reply, so they are mentally prepared for both and expect both to be a regular part of their schedule. It is within the context of a regularly occurring, predictable activity that students seem to become comfortable with their writing and open up and express themselves in writing the most freely.

CHAPTER 6

KEEPING IT GOING: STRATEGIES FOR MAINTAINING THE DIALOGUE

... the dream of liberating education is for equality and against hierarchy ... for an egalitarian classroom and against authoritarian relations in the classroom; for dialogue among peer students and with the teacher and against the monologue of the talking teacher who lectures students into silence and boredom.

Ira Shor, 1986, p. 5.

I think that the teacher's response should be as prompt as possible and something that's interesting. I've seen teachers' responses that just restate what the child has said, but do not add anything that's interesting for them to read. I think that instead, we need to always have some new, interesting information in our response.

Kelly Miller, 4th–6th grade ESL teacher

The most important thing to remember about the dialogue journal is that it is a wonderful opportunity to *have* an actual dialogue. It provides an alternative to much classroom oral interaction in which the teacher asks questions for the student to answer. It is also an alternative to writing assignments in which the student produces a written text and the teacher responds with brief, evaluative comments. The value of a journal is in the open and mutual exchange of ideas. The teacher has the chance to go beyond "being the teacher" and to share experiences, thoughts, and feelings.

Keeping the Conversation Going

Just as in oral, face-to-face conversation, creating a stimulating, ongoing dialogue can take time as participants seek to discover what

61

interests they have in common. Communication may seem somewhat awkward or difficult until the teacher and students get to know each other and become involved in mutually interesting topics. When students have been conditioned in school to answer questions and contribute little more to a discussion, it may be even more difficult. However, when teachers are simply responsive to what students have written, affirm them, and express interest in them as individuals and in what they are doing, communication begins to occur. Below are interactions from the first day of school between Leslee Reed and two of her sixth grade students learning English. Her responses make it clear that she respects and is interested in them and wants to know more about them.

Gloria: Today I was glad that I bring my lunch. Because I don't like the school turkey. Today I like geography because I like to look at maps to find direction of place.

Teacher: Yes! You were smart to have brought your lunch. That way you don't have to stand in line for 20 minutes.
Maps are fun. Did you like doing the map of our room? Was it hard?
I do hope you weren't hurt during our game time today!

* * * * * *

Antonio: 1. I am really interested in the book I have because I like baseball and now I know more about it.
2. In Geography we learned about land shapes.
3. We had a game for P.E.

Teacher: Terrific! I could see, Antonio, that you like baseball. Are the Dodgers your favorite team?
You seem interested in all of our lessons. It is great to have you in Room 11—you're a good student.

One way to generate a good discussion is to make contributions rather than to simply ask questions. Relating an experience, or telling about something you have been thinking about that is similar to an experience or thought the student has just told you about, often sparks student interest (only you can decide how personal you want to become when talking about yourself). Most experienced dialogue journal teachers agree that when they simply ask a lot of questions (a pattern that teachers are very comfortable with in the classroom and sometimes initially carry over to their journal writing), the interaction quickly becomes teacher-generated. The teacher defines the topics for discussion and the student's responses become brief answers to the questions, with little or no further information (cf. Hall & Duffy, 1987; Peyton & Seyoum, 1989, for discussion). Of course it is permissible to ask some questions, for they can help to sustain and encourage the written conversation. But giving information and stating an opinion along with asking a question gives students more to work with. In the two dialogue journal conversations that open this handbook, Mrs. Reed asks very few questions. When she does, they are usually embedded in other text. When the interaction patterns in her dialogue journals with her class of sixth graders learning English were analyzed (Peyton & Seyoum, 1989), it was found that she simply asked questions, without providing any other information, only around 10% of the time. Most of the time that she asked questions, she made contributions of her own as well (around 30% of the time). The majority of her writing (around 60% of the time) consisted of statements— information, opinions, observations. Rather than simply eliciting student writing, she was participating as a fellow writer herself.

As mentioned earlier, the writing should be adapted to the interests and language ability of individual students, as is done in oral conversation. The first-day responses to Gloria and Antonio above are as different as Gloria's and Antonio's entries. In Chapter 3 we showed how the language used with different students varied depending on the students' level of English proficiency as manifested in their writing. This individualization is not something that needs to be carefully worked on, but often comes naturally as teachers attempt to make themselves understood and to promote the writing of their students.

The most important overall strategy for the teacher is to enter into the journal interaction as a good conversationalist and an interesting writer, expect the students to do the same, and relax and enjoy the writing. Reading and writing in dialogue journals can be the best part of the day, a time to find out about those people you're spending the semester or year with and reflect with them on issues that are important to both of you.

Beyond maintaining a good conversation, a number of other issues inevitably come up once teachers have established a regular routine of dialogue journal writing:

- how to fit writing to individual students into an already busy schedule;
- whether and how to correct the students' writing;
- how to help students who can't think of things to write about;
- how to keep the writing from becoming too personal;
- and how to maintain students' privacy.

Finding Time for the Dialogue

There is no way around it; it takes time to read and respond thoughtfully to students' entries, especially when classes are large. The time factor is important because most teachers are busy already. Teachers who have experienced success with dialogue journals over extended periods of time have found ways to make the activity manageable. (See suggestions in "With whom to write" in Chapter 5). The key is to find a management pattern that suits the individual teacher's goals, personality, and situation.

Many teachers have reported that rather than being a burden, the time spent writing in journals is time well used. They gain valuable knowledge about students' interests and problems, receive feedback about the day's activities and lessons which can serve as the basis for future planning, and even find themselves refreshed by the dialogue. Nancie Atwell, for example, writes,

> I love to read and respond to their [students'] letters. It never seems a chore. I never know what I'll find when I turn to the last letter. I remember suffering through piles of junior high book reports, the dullest writing I've ever read. By contrast, kids' letters are a constant source of pleasure, surprise, and stimulation. And what they replaced—book reports, work sheets, quizzes, and tests—ate up more of my time than keeping up with my seventy-five correspondents ever will (1987, p. 194).

Leslee Reed describes her experience this way:

> Some people ask whether . . . writing in 26 journals is very tiring. I suppose, like everyone else, teaching exhausts me, but when I sit down to do my journals, I get rejuvenated. I get greatly amused at some of the comments the children make. Sometimes their advice to me is hilarious. Their feedback is so good for me and I really look forward to it. I can be just dog tired and think, "Well, I've got to get back to my journals," and the first thing I know, I'm so involved that I'm no longer weary. It's a good way for me to go (1988, p. 71).

Those teachers who find the writing worthwhile for them and their students have decided to continue with dialogue journals, regardless of the time it takes.

> If I thought that this was a chore, I wouldn't do it. You have to be able to convey to the students that this is something that is enjoyable, that you enjoy doing it and they will enjoy it too, so they will dive in.
>
> Dawn Center, 1st and 2nd grade ESL teacher

There is no question that this procedure, of reading and replying to each entry daily, is time-consuming. Is it worthwhile, however, in terms of accomplishing the goals I and my students have? Yes, yes, a thousand times yes.

Harriet Hulings, 9th–12th grade ESL teacher[6]

Correcting the Writing

One of the central tenets of dialogue journal writing has been that students' writing should not be overtly corrected. The teacher may model some of the words and structures used incorrectly by the student, but the teacher's contribution to the journal is a genuine message, a response to the content rather than a comment on the form of the student's writing. However, some students are concerned about the correctness of their writing and want correction in the journal. This seems to be especially true of older students. Paul Jones (1988) found in a study of adult ESL students that almost all of the beginning students and half of the advanced students wanted their errors corrected. One expressed the following view:

I want to be corrected. I don't think I'll learn anything like this. Of course I make mistakes, and if I don't get corrected I'll make mistakes again and again. I don't write anything I think is wrong. When I write I think it's right, but maybe it's not. That's why I want it to be corrected.

It is important to discuss this desire with students so they don't experience continued frustration if error correction is a concern for them. The goals of the journal writing and the reasons for not correcting errors within the dialogue need to be made very clear. Teachers might also find ways to address errors without disturbing the flow of the dialogue. They might, for example, tell students that if they mark in their entry a particular word or structure they are unsure about, the teacher will attempt to use that word or structure in the response. Parts of students' entries might be copied, discussed, and corrected in individual student-teacher conferences, or errors that occur in many students' writing might be discussed with the whole class. Jones (1988) discusses use by some teachers of a "grammatical P.S." At the end of a response, the teacher adds a gentle P.S. on one or two specific points: "By the way, in English we usually say . . . ." A teacher in Japan reserves a part of the blackboard for dialogue journal "hints," which are changed every few days. Many of the hints concern possible things to write about, but some focus on formal aspects of writing.

---

[6]From a paper written for a graduate course in ESL.

For example, "When you write the speech of the teacher or your friends, are you putting quotation marks? If you do, the meaning will be clearer and it will be easier to read" (Kitagawa & Kitagawa, 1987, p. 64).

Students need other opportunities—revised and edited essays, for example—to receive feedback on the correctness of their writing. If they are confident they will receive such feedback elsewhere, they might not feel the need for it in their journals.

Finding Topics to Write About

Many teachers have wondered whether they should assign topics for writing. As discussed earlier, in some instances the teacher might want the writing to focus on topics or issues related to the content of the class; for example, reflections on readings and authors in a literature class, or exploration of new insights in a science, math, history, or social studies class. However, beyond the overall instruction to "write about what you are learning in this class," most teachers have found that it is best to let the dialogue remain open-ended and flexible. In fact, they find that students often intersperse comments about personal issues and concerns with discussions of course content without losing sight of the goal of the journals, and that this freedom enhances the quality of the discussion. (Samway, 1989, found through trial and error that blocking the expression of personal issues can seriously stifle the dialogue.) A set of topics outlined ahead of time risks turning the journal into simply another writing assignment and could block the slow evolution of topics that can occur in a good discussion.

Sometimes, especially early in the year or semester, students don't know what to write about. Together, the class can brainstorm possible topics or entries and even come up with some entries that can be copied by those who don't know what to write. One year, Mrs. Reed's sixth grade students collaboratively produced this sample entry for the first day of writing, which fit her minimum three-sentence requirement.

> It is the first day of school in Room 11. I'm in the sixth grade and my teacher is Mrs. Reed. Today was a hot and humid day.

Of her 26 students, only three simply copied the three sentences and wrote nothing else. Others used parts of it and added their own ideas, and others created their entire entry themselves, ignoring the sample. But it gave a start to those who needed it. The important thing is that everyone had something to write and felt comfortable with it.

The journal writing "hints" in the corner of the Japanese teacher's blackboard, mentioned earlier, are sometimes designed to help students find something to write about. The hints might suggest possible topics, ask questions about an activity the students are engaged in, ask students to analyze classroom behavior, or include sample entries from former students (Kitagawa & Kitagawa, 1987, p. 64).

Keeping the Writing from Becoming Too Personal

Some teachers are afraid that leaving the choice of topics entirely open to students encourages them to write about very personal topics or family affairs that the teacher is not prepared to deal with, and that the writing can turn into a counseling session. This does occur at times. However, it need not continue. Teachers can gently point out that they are not comfortable discussing that topic and introduce another one. One elementary teacher tells her students at the beginning of the year that the intention of the journal is not to share secrets or to delve into her or the students' private lives. It is for discussing things they are doing at home, at school, with friends, and things they are thinking about that aren't secrets.

At the same time, knowledge about personal issues may be valuable to the teacher and can be handled effectively in the journal. For example, one of Mrs. Reed's sixth grade students told her about a couple of other girls who were planning to run away. Without breaking the writer's confidence, Mrs. Reed was able to offer to help.

Elizabeth: What would you do if someone you knew was running away. They had the money to go to San Francisco or San Diego. They had about $1,000. You had already tried to convince them to stay but they still were going to. Would you tell their parents? What would you do?

Teacher: That is a serious problem. Have you discussed it with your Mother? If she knows the people involved she may have an idea. If it is someone here at school, someone your Mother doesn't know well, you would be wise to tell Mrs. F____. Running away is an extremely dangerous thing to do. I hope you see that they get help.

Elizabeth: The only thing is, I don't want her to hate me afterward. Actually its 2 girls that are running away. Yesterday she stayed after school and I tryed to talk her out of it. She kept on saying "My parents ruined my life."

Teacher: I am very concerned about the girls' running away. If you still feel they are about to do that kind of thing, would you want me to ask Mrs. F____ to speak to them? I do feel we *must* do something if they are determined to take this kind of action.

Elizabeth: It's Ellen that's running away. Has Dena already told you? What are you going to do?

Teacher: Yes, I know who it is and am pleased because I really think I may be able to help. I won't ever tell what I know or who told me. I will begin at once to see what I can do.

If the problem is beyond the teacher's expertise, it is wise to refer the student to another source of help—a counselor or parent.

The personal quality of the writing is really up to the teacher, who must decide what the goal is for the writing and what level of sharing feels comfortable.

Maintaining Privacy

Most teachers and students agree that the journal communication is a private dialogue, to be shared with other teachers, students, or parents only at the discretion of the student. Students should be assured of the privacy of their writing from the beginning, but advised that if they should write in the journal about a danger to themselves or another student, or about something that requires intervention, someone will need to be informed. In such a case it is best to discuss the situation with the student first if possible, so as not to lose trust or betray a confidence.

It may be that others—other students, other teachers, a parent, or an administrator—want to read a particular student's journal. Some students want to share their writing with others and should be free to choose to do so. But the reading of a student's journal should never be allowed without that student's permission. This can be avoided by not leaving journals unattended on desks or shelves and by keeping them locked up when not in students' possession.

Teachers need to make it a policy not to discuss students' journal entries in the teachers' lounge or in teachers' meetings. If the journals are used for research purposes or if samples are pulled for presentation to others, student permission (as well as parent permission, when appropriate) must be obtained and anonymity assured. (As it turned out, many of the students whose writing is shown in this handbook wanted their real names used.)

CHAPTER 7

WHAT TO DO IF . . . : STRATEGIES FOR HANDLING PROBLEMS

This work is not unlike making stone walls, by piling one rock on another, but the more steady, detailed, and continuous that piling is, the more certain is the strength, and the less likely to tumble down.

Japanese educator, quoted in Kitagawa and Kitagawa, 1987, p. 63

In this chapter some strategies are suggested for handling commonly occurring problems, from working with the student who is reluctant to write, to understanding and responding to the student whose entries are indecipherable. Ways of handling specific situations cannot, of course, be prescribed or decided upon ahead of time, because they are integrally tied to particular situations or students, or even the time of year. These suggestions are therefore very general and can be adapted as appropriate.

Writing with the Reluctant Writer

Not all students are enthusiastic about dialogue journal writing. Some may fulfill the requirements to write, but make their reluctance to communicate obvious by writing the absolute minimum amount possible, writing nearly the same thing every day, and ignoring what the teacher writes. Raoul, a sixth grader from Mexico, was one such student in Leslee Reed's class. All of his entries in October, November, and December were very similar, much like those shown below.

October
> Raoul: I hope we have a nice day today Mrs. reed and I hope we have P.E. and I hope we have a nice ricese and a nice lunch time and a good playtime.

November

Raoul: I wish we have a good day and I hope we have a good lunch time today and recess time I hope theres no trouble today.

Teacher: You were angry with me this morning. You are not at school to play—even art is a way to learn. We measured and used a ruler to help us learn.

Raoul: I hope we have a good time today and a good recess a good lunch time and a good playtime. I hope we wont get in any trouble.

Teacher: I am sorry you wrote this and did not keep your journal with you. You could help me so much if you would tell me in your journal why you are having trouble. I would like to make school easier for you by helping to solve some problems.

Raoul: I hope we have a nice day today and a good recess time and a good lunch time . . .

Writing with Raoul was an extremely frustrating experience. He continued to write nearly the same thing each day for almost the entire year, glossing over the real problems he was having in class and making it clear that he was not interested in communicating. Mrs. Reed wrote back each day, trying to vary her response, affirm him, and find something that might interest him. She also tried to address problems he was having and offer help. Primarily, she tried to keep the channel of communication open, in case Raoul ever did decide he wanted to communicate.

Finally, very late in the year, some difficult events occurred, and the written interaction offered a way for Raoul to handle them. For example, when the class was planning to go to the local Junior High for an orientation trip, Raoul never returned his permission slip allowing him to go. When Mrs. Reed asked him about it, he explained his predicament in the journal, and they worked out a solution together.

Raoul: . . . and you know why I don't want to go to Virgil because I had three girl friends there and they thought I was going to King J.H. and if they see me they are going to be very mad. I hope I don't have to go with you.

Teacher: No! I did not know that you had told anyone that you were in Junior High. I'm glad you told me. I understand the problem. If they saw you with the 6th graders they would know you had been giving them a line! I will see what I can arrange.

Raoul: Thanks a lot I really apprisiated. If I don't go were am I staying will you tell me please. . . I hope you guys have a good time at Virgil thats to bad I can't go.

This event and the discussion around it initiated a genuine interaction that continued for the rest of the year. Raoul still had days when he returned to his repetitive writing about recess and lunch, but he also wrote about real events in his life, making it possible for genuine discussions to occur, and in some cases, for potential problems to be averted ahead of time. By the end of the year, he and Mrs. Reed had developed a genuine friendship.

Kitagawa and Kitagawa (1987, pp. 62–64) describe a teacher in Japan (Kamemura) who requires not that children write, but that they turn in their journals on a schedule whether or not they have written anything. Kamemura writes to each child anyway, and has found that "few children can resist writing at least a line or two after reading about three of these messages" (p. 63). Kamemura admits that it is sometimes difficult to write to a child who is not writing, but explains that he writes about important aspects of the child's life, things he might say anyway if he and the child talked. His challenge is to think of some area of the child's experience in which they have something in common and in which the child is interested.

Even Kamemura has children "who are so thick-skinned as to resist writing while enjoying his comments anyway" (p. 63). With those children he uses the journal as an opportunity for giving guidance, and finds that they are always eager to read what he has written even if they don't write.

Raoul's story had a happy ending and Kamemura has worked out an approach to journal writing that seems to fulfill his and his students' needs. But some students may never come to enjoy the journal. That is their choice. Just as dialogue journals are not enjoyed by all teachers, they are not enjoyed by all students.

Writing with the Repetitive Writer

The early writing of many ESL students can be very repetitive, because they repeatedly use in their journals language patterns and routines they have learned and feel comfortable with in speech. For example, many low-proficiency students write endless variations on an "I like" pattern, as did Ruqayya, a fourth grader from Pakistan, and José, a sixth grader from El Salvador.

Ruqayya: I like to fly.
            I like school.
            I like to play.
            I don't lik fish.
            I like this day.

* * * * * *

José: do you like Halloween. I like Halloween are you watching
       Mr T I like Mr. T do you like Mr. T

Patterns like these can become a very comfortable, safe way for a beginning writer to get something in print. Students sometimes seem to reach a level of certainty with parts of the language that they know and do not progress further. However, the patterns can become a crutch that is difficult to drop, but must be dropped so the writer can move into more creative language use.

The teacher can use various strategies to help students move out of using such fixed language patterns. He or she can vary, build on, or extend the pattern the student used, by adding details to it, by changing the order of the patterns, or by introducing new patterns related to new topics. For example, when the student writes something like "I like the game," the teacher might add a detail about the game and an additional comment: "I can see you like the handball game. You were playing so hard!" Time or location could be added: "Yes, you liked the game we played at recess" or "You liked the game we played with the other class." Revising the structure of the statement can help to change the pattern while using the same, familiar vocabulary: "We played a lot of games. It looked like you liked the handball game the best." The teacher can also ask a question to encourage the student to elaborate: "Those *were* great games. Which ones did you like best?"

With more advanced students, the teacher may simply want to respond briefly to the student's topic and then introduce other topics, thus modeling variation and creativity.

Students can also be encouraged to write about texts they are reading, which often become valuable resources of new words or structures.

It is possible that students who continue writing fixed language patterns and routines are not reading the teacher's entries, and they may need to be encouraged to do so. By varying their own writing, teachers can give students a daily model of what can be done in writing, but the students must read the teacher's entry to benefit.

Writing with the Student Who Has "Nothing to Write About"

Once students become accustomed to writing regularly to a known audience, they learn to choose aspects of their own lives, their readings, topics they are studying in school, or societal issues that are worth writing about. However, there will inevitably be days when topics for discussion are exhausted, nothing major is happening, and students can't think of anything to write about. On these days they may simply need to write the minimum, maybe a diary-like review of their day, and wait for a more productive and interesting day. But there are some ways to help the blocked writer. Sometimes just talking briefly with the teacher about what they've been doing, books they've been reading, or things they've been thinking about can spark ideas. Students can also be reminded that rereading the teacher's last entry may give them ideas. Are there any things in the teacher's entry that are worth writing more about? Are there any questions that need to be answered or any questions the students might want to ask about that entry? The teacher's writing can be an important model of topics that are worth writing about and of ways of writing that are interesting, lively, and varied, and it is helpful if students come to recognize it as a resource.

With all three kinds of students discussed above—the reluctant, repetitive, and blocked writer—a great deal of patience may be required, for it may take a long time before they respond to the dialogue journal idea and begin to write substantive, interesting entries. Some may never get to that point. With some students, especially those who are having problems in other areas of school as well, the fact that they are writing anything in their dialogue journal may be a victory.

Responding to Entries That Are Difficult to Decipher

The entries of some students at the beginning stages of learning English may be so difficult to read, because of handwriting and spelling, that the teacher has little idea of what they have written. To address this problem very beginning writers might read the entry aloud to the teacher or an aide (described in the section in Chapter 4 on "Beginning writers"). But when students become more independent, such oral explanations usually do not take place during class, and the teacher is left to decipher the entry without help. The writing of Su Kyong, a sixth grader from Korea, shown in Figure 13, is an example of such an entry. It appears she is reporting that she came to school, telling about a trip to Japanese Town and about her math class, and saying that her head hurts ("my had is hord little"). The teacher works with what she can read, along with her knowledge about Su Kyong (she knows that she missed a day of school because of a headache), to compose her response:

> I am glad you are back. I missed you so much. I like to go to Japanese Town, too. Did you eat there? I hope your head does not hurt. I miss you. At noon

Figure 13

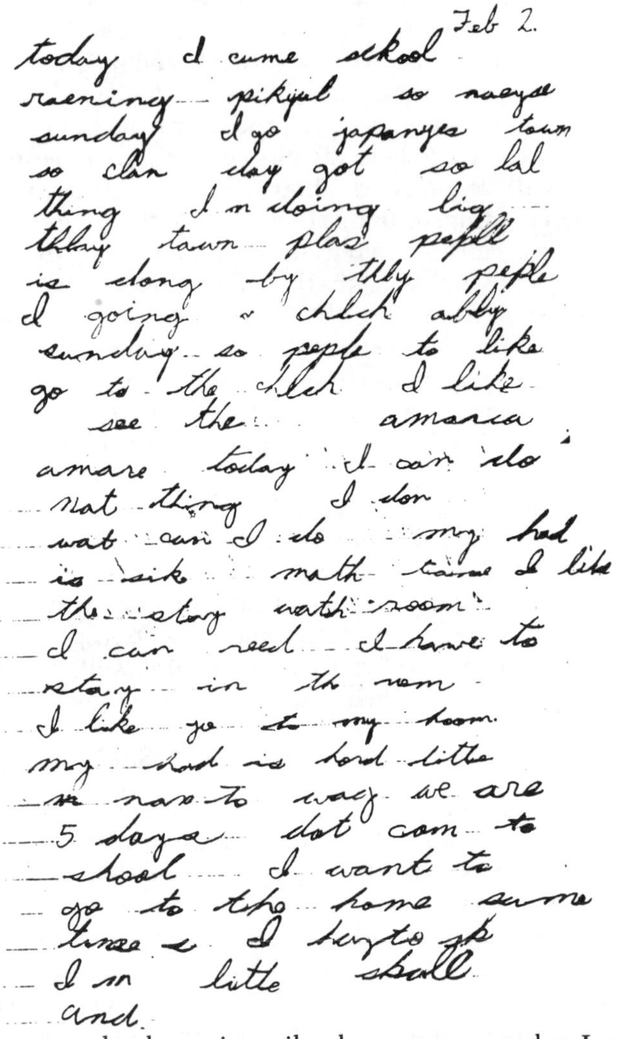

today I cume sckool raening pikyul so naeyse sunday I go japanyes town so clan day got so lal thing Im doing big thlay town plas pepll is dong by thly peple I going chlch ably sunday so peple to like to to the chlch I like see the amarca amare today I can do not thing I don wat can I do my had is sik math time I like the story wath room I can reed I have to stay in the rom I like go to my room. My had is hord litle nax to wag we are 5 days dot come to shool I want to go to the home some sume time s I hayto sk Im litle skull and

I had a meeting and I could not let boys and girls come in. You can come in on Tuesday noon.

If an entry is completely indecipherable, the teacher can simply write, "I didn't understand what you wrote today. Will you please explain it to me again?"

If students are attempting new structures that they have not yet mastered, their imperfect use of these structures may result in a message that is somewhat garbled and difficult to understand, as shown in an entry by Michael, a sixth grader from Burma, in Figure 14. Michael had been writing in English for five months and was now attempting to use more complex structures. A teacher who dismissed the entry as incomprehensible would miss the fact that Michael was making an important point and giving good reasons for his request. It is crucial that such clear thinking not be missed or diminished because of muddled structures. Before responding, the teacher might restate mentally, as closely as possible, what the student has written. This assures that it is understood, and that the response is appropriate and consistent with the student's level of thought. Michael's entry can be restated thus:

> . . . will you tell Mrs. P [Mrs. P is the reading specialist, who came once a week] not to come on Tuesday, because you have yard duty and a meeting after school. I want her to come on Monday instead, so she won't have to leave so soon, she can stay after school longer, and we can talk about the reading.

This is the teacher's response:

> . . . Yes, I will tell Mrs. P. You do have good ideas. May I show her what you wrote? I am sure she will be interested. We all like to talk about all of the books we are reading!

Whatever the causes of difficulty with reading students' journal entries, students are probably trying to express ideas that are important to them. Those ideas need to be respected, and teachers need to make every attempt to understand and respond.

Addressing Behavior Problems

The journal is a good place to address problems that students are having in school, because the privacy of the writing allows discussion toward a solution without disruption of the entire class, and because both student and teacher have time to reflect on the problem as they

Figure 14

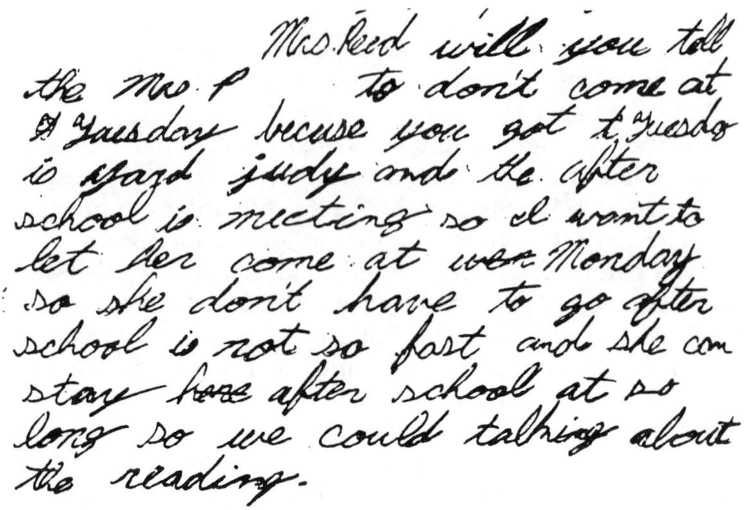

> ... Mrs. Reed will you tell the Mrs. P to don't come at Tuesday because you got Tuesday is yard duty and the after school is meeting so I want to let her come at Monday so she don't have to go after school is not so fast and she can stay after school at so long so we could talking about the reading.

make their statements and argue their points. Some very valuable discussions of behavior problems can take place in the journal. For example, Jung An, a sixth grader from Korea, was an advanced, motivated student, but at one point in the year he stopped working hard and began getting low grades. His performance was often the topic of long discussions in his journal:

Jung An: Did you did as you promised me, did you start over my grade? I hope you did. Gosh you took me by the suprise about report card. boy am I nervous well have a nice day.

Teacher: I cannot re-do your grade unless you re-do your work. I can understand why you are nervous. You have done less than average work. I remember telling the class several times that the ocean report would be the main part of your mid-March report card.

Jung An: Yes I understand anyhow I really didn't did my best. I think I will have to explain my dad I didn't did my best. Boy was I nervous when my dad came to the class. fortunately he came to get the key.

Teacher: You know you did not do your best so I'm sure the grade on your report was no surprise. I do hope that you will try a lot harder. You are a very bright boy who sometimes just doesn't want to pay attention.

Jung An: Mrs. Reed guess what I can't believe my eyes when my dad took it so naturally about my report card.
    I know and now I will do my best because I have someone to compete.

Teacher: Your Dad is very smart! He knows what you do at home so he probably was not surprised, because he knows you were not listening at school.
    I really hope you do try harder. Your fine brain is just resting and not working for you.

In discussions like these, teachers have the opportunity to describe situations as they see them, affirm students and their ability to do well, and offer a plan of action.

We saw earlier how Mrs. Reed and Raoul worked through an awkward situation, a field trip he did not want to take, without involving others in the class. Later in the year, Mrs. Reed was able to foresee and possibly prevent a problem at the school's graduation ceremonies:

Teacher: Are your parents going to come to your promotion?

Raoul: No my parents arent going to come. some of my home boys [fellow gang members] are going to come because you don't know what may happen.

Teacher: What do you mean by "you don't know what may happen"? We've been doing this for years and nothing happens! We all have a good time and you get your promotion after the ceremony. So if anything happens during the ceremony—you may not get your promotion. I'm glad your friends want to come—but they can cause you a problem, too.

Raoul: No they wont their already vets they have babies they wont start nothing. only if some one comes up to them. there just going to site down and watch.

Oral follow-up may be required in some situations, but in many, the problem can be taken care of entirely in the journal.

Responding to Angry Entries

The dialogue journal is also a good place for students to vent their emotions, which may include anger. They don't usually do this until later in the year, after they have passed through the polite, superficial "I love math and I love you" stage of the interaction and have begun to express their true feelings. Again, the ability to pour out their emotions in the journal gives teacher and student the opportunity to discuss what is happening and what can be done about it without class disruptions. Benny, a sixth grader from Puerto Rico, was quick to express his negative reactions to whatever happened in class that displeased him. Here he expressed his anger about the advice Mrs. Reed had given him about his vulture for his social studies project.

> Benny: I have not read any of the stuff you wrote because I hate reading what you write to me. I am nearly done with the thing on the vulture. I hate the vulture. I made it the way you told me. Now it looks like a bird with a striped skirt on. I don't like it any more. I used to like it when there was no dum feathers on it. Now it looks so dum. Did you known that the same day I bought a record my brother broke it.

> Teacher: I wonder why you don't like what I write. I like what you write even if you are not in a good mood.
>   The head and neck of your vulture are particularly good. Why don't you look for a better picture of the feather placement? Have you found the size of the vulture?

Note that Benny ended his entry on a positive note. Mrs. Reed has found that once students have expressed their anger in the journal they no longer feel it so strongly, and she sees students busily erasing angry entries written earlier and writing new ones or adding something positive at the end, as Benny did. Mrs. Reed responded positively to Benny's outburst rather than "fighting back" and tried to offer suggestions for how he might improve his vulture, which had become a disappointment.

Major upheavals in students' lives, such as moving and attending another school, can lead to a sense of confusion and strong emotion, which sometimes is expressed as anger and even hatred:

> Alex: . . . I wish I didn't move but my mom wants to move because my family is over there at m____. I hope tomor-

> row I have fun because its going to be my last day . . . .
> I hate you miss reed ranold didn't even stay in at recess.
> its a good thing Im leaving. I hope theres no teacher like
> you at M_____ high school is ronald going to stay in for
> recess tomorrow because if he isn't he is going to get it.

Teacher: You were really angry. I'm glad you were willing to write
it! That isn't a fun way to feel. How can we keep you from
getting so upset? I'd be willing to help you plan a way.
> I will miss you. I still wish you could stay here until
school is out and then go to M_____! Sometimes we can't
do what we want to do.

Here it is obvious even from Alex's writing the conflicting feelings
he is having. This pattern has been so consistent in Mrs. Reed's work
with students of this age that she isn't thrown by the negative expression of feelings. Instead, she acknowledges and even identifies with
them.

It must be pointed out that Mrs. Reed had been writing in dialogue
journals with upper elementary school students for over 15 years
when she wrote the entries to Benny and Alex shown here. During this
time she tried, dropped, and improved on strategies for handling
problems and began to see rather predictable patterns emerge (like
the mixture of emotions during a time of personal change and upset)
that could be handled in tried and true ways. An examination of her
responses to angry students reveals that she tends to use the following
strategies:

- Responds as directly and honestly to the situation as possible,
  without making accusations;
- Acknowledges the anger and the reasons for it;
- Affirms the student and her liking for him or her;
- Offers options for future action or offers to help in some way.

A teacher new to dialogue journal writing may despair of ever being
able to respond in this way, and it may be that initial attempts are
disappointing. However, with time and practice at listening to students and attempting to communicate with them in an authentic,
constructive way, patterns will begin to become clear and successful
strategies will emerge.

Writing in the Student's Native Language

One issue that ESL teachers often mention is that students sometimes write in the dialogue journal in their native language. So far in

our experience, and that of other teachers, this has not been a problem. If teachers do not understand the student's language or have a classroom aide who does, they can let the student keep a personal journal in their native language until the student feels ready to write the dialogue in English. Teachers can explain that they don't understand the language and therefore, unfortunately, cannot write back.

However, if the teacher or an aide does understand the language and can write in it, the journal interaction can begin in that language, and the student can ease gradually into writing in English. There have been instances in which students produced very little writing in English, but when asked to write in their native language, wrote lengthy, interesting, and coherent pieces. The teachers were then able to build on their interest in writing and their ability to write and gradually move to writing in English (Carole Urzua, personal communication, April 1987). Students who started out writing in Spanish and made just such a transition to English without being asked to are described in Chapter 4 and in the student profiles in Chapter 8.

* * * * * *

Numerous other problems could be addressed, and individual teachers will have unique situations to work with. We have discussed here those problems that teachers have mentioned frequently, and have given some overall guidelines for addressing them and some illustrative examples of ways that Mrs. Reed has handled them in her writing with her students. We hope that these general guidelines and examples will be helpful in addressing these and other problems that may come up.

CHAPTER 8

PROFILES OF INDIVIDUAL STUDENT WRITERS

... each [student has] her or his own individual approach to the process of L2 learning, and this approach might change over time or in different situations. As teachers we accept each [student's] approach or style while we encourage all attempts to communicate.

Celia Genishi, 1989, p. 514

Elsewhere in this handbook we have presented personal examples of writing from different students' journals to illustrate various points, but have not looked at the development of individual writers during the course of a school year. In this section we present profiles of the development over time of individual students, representing different ages and levels of English proficiency. The intent in presenting profiles in this manner is to give an indication of the types of writing, patterns of development, and kinds of changes that teachers might expect from their own students. We hope that they also demonstrate clearly some of the benefits of dialogue journal writing we have described. The profiles, all of nonnative English speakers, move from younger to older students and from those who are less proficient to those who are more proficient with written English.

Catalina: Starting with Drawing

Many teachers working with adults and children have asked, "What if they don't yet know how to write? How can they keep a dialogue journal?" Any students, children or adults, can begin a dialogue journal as soon as they know some oral English and have some idea that marks on paper convey meaning. They do not need to have mastered the alphabet or the conventions of written English. These will develop

81

as they continue to write. They can begin by drawing a message that the teacher replies to, or dictating a message that the teacher writes and then replies to. Most students very quickly begin to write, often copying words from print materials in the classroom and gradually becoming more independent and producing longer and more varied messages. Catalina's work illustrates the development that is possible with students at this stage.

Catalina, whose journal writing is shown elsewhere in this handbook, was a first grader in Ruth Sedei's combined first and second grade class of nonnative English speakers. She was a native Spanish speaker from Colombia and had been in the United States only one year when school began. She spoke Spanish at home, had attended a Spanish-speaking preschool, and began the year with very little English.

Like the other students in her class, Catalina began writing in her dialogue journal after about a month of school. By that time she had learned school routines and some oral English, knew how to produce English letters, but had had very little experience with writing in English. Therefore, she started out by drawing and labeling pictures, as in the example in Figure 15a. Most of the time she asked for help with every word she wrote, or found and copied words from the print that was plentiful in the room or previous journal entries. The teacher wrote a reply, building on the picture or the labels.

Catalina eventually began to write simple sentences (Figure 15b) and even more complex messages (Figure 15c). This writing was always copied or done with a lot of help. For example, for the entry in Figure 15b she copied Monica's name from her desk and asked for help writing the rest of her message.

For over half of the year, until well into March, Catalina was reluctant to write anything without help. She was determined that her writing would be perfectly correct, and even though she was urged to attempt to write independently, her writing time was spent moving from resource to resource, from people to books and other print, looking for help. She had many human resources to choose from—the teacher, an aide, a researcher[7], and a best friend. As a result, her spelling was always correct, as she wanted it to be. When Mrs. Sedei, attempting to develop more independence in all of the children, decided they could ask for help with only one word a day (which they wrote in their self-made dictionaries), Catalina was quite upset and worked with her friend Monica, one of the most advanced children in the class and also a Spanish speaker, as much as she could.

---

[7]Joy Peyton did research for a year in this class.

Figure 15a

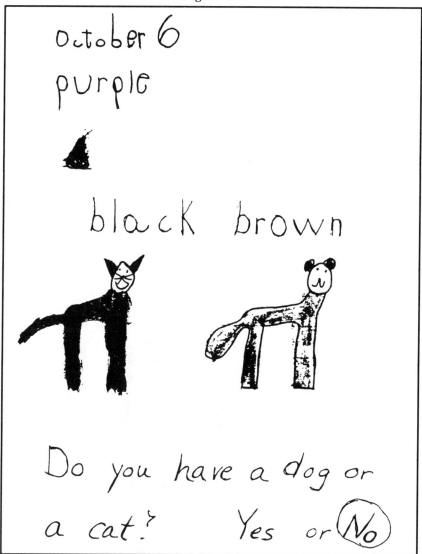

In March, after considerable prodding and encouragement from her parents and Mrs. Sedei, Catalina became convinced that she could write independently, and she began to sound out the words she wanted to write and experiment with spellings. In Figure 15d, for example, she copied "Friday" and "Today" from the class calendar and bulletin board, and wrote the rest herself.

This step away from standard English spelling was a positive one

October 29

Monica and LιReMilK

I drink milk for dinner.
I drink juice for breakfast.

Figure 15c

November 18
my father is happy
because I read the
book to him

I am happy too.

You can read many words

for Catalina. Once she was willing to break away from the crutch of constant assistance and risk writing on her own, she was free to write about whatever she wanted to. She was no longer confined to short, perfect messages or words she could find in the room and her books. She began to write about the world beyond herself and the classroom (Figure 15e), about past events (Figure 15f), and future plans (Figure 15g), nearly always accompanying her written entry with an illustration. She also began to write more extended texts, including an explanation for her behavior (Figure 15h) and a narrative of an experience (Figure 15i).

Finally, near the end of the year, she began to show awareness of Mrs. Sedei as her reader. This is something that does not seem to happen until near the end of the first grade, if it happens then, at least in Mrs. Sedei's experience. Many of her first graders wrote self-contained entries in their dialogue journals all year, without acknowledging her writing to them. Catalina followed the same pattern until May, when she began to acknowledge Mrs. Sedei as a fellow writer—asking questions and answering them (Figure 15j–1 & 2), addressing her directly or referring to her, and sharing experiences (Figure 15k).

During the year, Catalina's journal writing developed remarkably in a number of ways. She moved from drawing and single words, to sentences copied from words in the room, to writing independently

March 20

Friday I pie a psow
the psow is red
an Today I pie
a Crayons to

I didn't see your new red
pencil. I did see your
Crayons. Now you can do goodwork.

March 20
Friday I buy a pencil
The pencil is red.
And today I buy crayons too.

[Mrs. Sedei, who is accustomed to reading children's writing, provided these "translations."]

April 3
Today mo car es prken I am sad pboss ma co r dasant work

I hope your father got your broken car fixed. Something is wrong with my car too. It says, "Hm-m-m-m-m!"

April 3
Today my car is broken. I am sad because my car doesn't work.

March 24

thes mone I look at a car hit a cat the litte cat die

That is so sad. Did you cry when the car hit the cat? I know I would have cried— The poor little cat.

March 24
This morning I saw a car hit a cat. The little cat died.

March 25

Aftrnw ma mother

es god to help min

Spelling List

Your mother is nice to help you study for your spelling test. You will do a good job.

March 25

This afternoon my mother is going to help me [my?] spelling list.

May 14

Mrs. Sedei I tavesave

I cam laet I Not No

wie I cam laet I

dad t he thans hard my

sas tr Not dwthe thans

have that was my Siste

fal becas my Siste Not

harve

I know it is not your fault

that you are late. I really

think that you should ride

the bus. Then you could always

May 14

Mrs. Sedei, I am very sorry I came late. I don't know why I came late. I did the things [in a hurry?]. My sister did not do the things [in a hurry?]. That was my sister's fault, because my sister did not hurry.

May 18

My mother fan had a
bae in sunday the bae
is a gir. Hr is. pate. Hr was
sleep and I caft hr a bed
to sleep and Sanday the sam
bae I see he.

You gave the baby a carseat.
All babies need to sit in a car
seat. It makes the baby safe
in the car.
What is the name
of your friend's
baby?

May 18
My mother's friend had a baby on Sunday. The baby is a girl.
She is pretty. She was sleeping and I gave her a bed to sleep on
and Sunday the same day I saw her.

Figure 15j-1

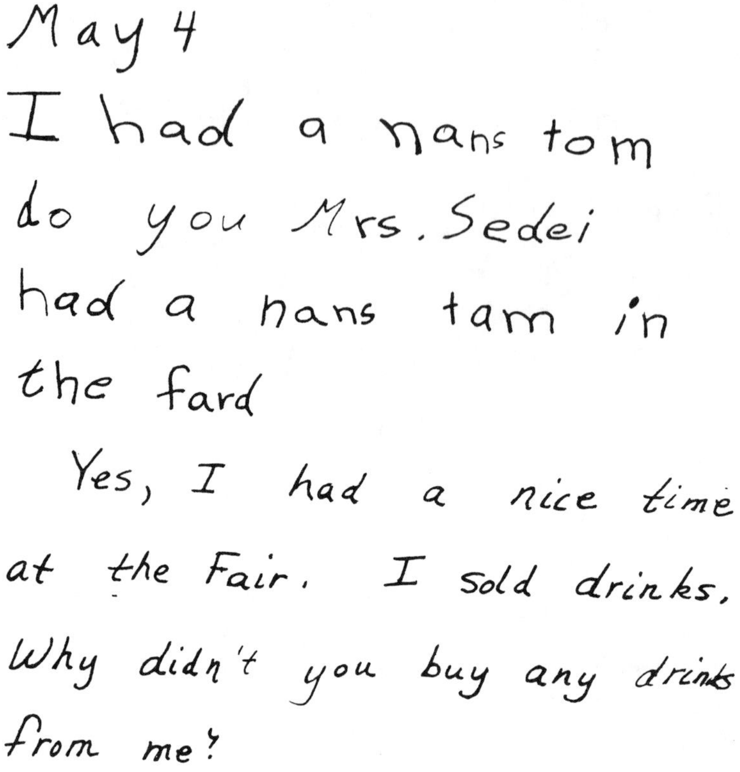

May 4

I had a nans tom
do you Mrs. Sedei
had a nans tam in
the fard

Yes, I had a nice time
at the Fair. I sold drinks.
Why didn't you buy any drinks
from me?

May 4
I had a nice time. Did you, Mrs. Sedei, have a nice time at the
fair?

with invented spelling; from one-proposition statements to a variety
of types of extended texts, including narrations and explanations (her
journal averaged 5 words per entry in October and November and 28
words per entry in May and June); from simple to more complex
sentence structures; from a focus on the "here and now," herself and
her own feelings and current activities, to a focus on past and future
events in which others were involved; from simply writing to writing
for a recognized audience; and from self-contained entries to continued conversations. She still needed to develop standard writing conventions, but that could come later.

As she saw herself develop, Catalina was delighted (along with

Figure 15j-2

May 5

becas we Not wat to las
ar taes af sat becus
We NOt Wat to las
ar tacs sube my
Mothre Not wat

I think it was because
you weren't thirsty. I
understand. What did you
use your tickets for?

May 5
Because we did not want to lose our tickets . . .

Mrs. Sedei) with her progress and her sense of independence, as they expressed in this exchange:

April 10

Catalina: I am hap bPeKas I bu ma wok pae mo saf an Mrs. Sedei to is hap
[I am happy because I do my work by myself and Mrs. Sedei is happy too.]

beautiful too.

Are you going to go swimming tomorrow? I need a new bathing suit.

May 22

Wal af tasan fat ca me and I wal ca my mother af you can cat anw pdnsud I wal cat you a has pednswt

Thank-you for wanting to help me find a bathing suit that fits. If I don't find a bathing suit. I can sit at the side of my pool and put my feet in the water

Have a good weekend!

May 22

Well, if it doesn't fit, tell me and I will tell my mother if you can get a new bathing suit. I will get you a nice bathing suit.

Teacher: Catalina, I am so proud of you. I told you that you could do your work by yourself. Now you do. You are ready to be in second grade next year.

Catalina's development was, of course, not confined to her journal writing. By the end of the year she was keeping book and science journals, writing letters to other students and teachers, and creating imaginative stories. When Joy Peyton asked her in an interview whether she thought she had improved during the year, she said proudly that before she was scared to write and always asked for help with everything. But now she was a good writer, and when she didn't know how to write something she figured it out herself. She was ready for the second grade.

Miguel: The Development of English Fluency

Miguel, a fifth grader in Kelly Miller's fourth through sixth grade ESL class, started school immediately after arriving from El Salvador, knowing no English. Miguel represents those students discussed earlier who need individualized instruction but often do not get it, because they are in classes with many other students who are functioning at a much more advanced level of English proficiency and have their own needs. The teacher and classroom aide (if the class is fortunate enough to have one) are already very busy and not able to spend a lot of time with one student.

Because Miguel was one of two new students who knew no English, in a class of 16 nonnative English speakers, he often looked scared, lost, and lonely, and remained very quiet. For the first several months he and the other new student, Mario, either worked separately with the classroom aide or worked together in workbooks designed by the county for beginning English learners. (The workbook exercises began with color- and shape-matching activities and moved to word- and sentence-copying, fill-in-the blanks, and pattern drills—"Is John a teacher?" The student answers, "No, he's not."; "Are you a teacher?" "No, I'm not."; etc.) When speaking with Miguel or Mario individually, Mrs. Miller and the aide often spoke Spanish. By the end of the year these students had become more integrated into the regular activities of the classroom and even joined reading and writing groups with other students, but Miguel talked in class only when asked a question.

Like the other students in his class, Miguel began writing in his journal on the first day of school. His first entry was written in very limited Spanish:

September 2

Miguel: tedo uno ermana i un ermado tedo a mi mami i a mi popi. yo cotodos. Eyos vi mi felis a mi casa i ti i mi tilla. lego to dos domigo.

Teacher: Tu tienes un hermano, una hermana, tu mamá y tu papá. Ustedes son muy felices en tu casa. Tu tío y tía llegaron los domingos. ¿Es lo que me dijiste? Yo tengo 2 hermanos, 3 hermanas, mi papá y mamá. También, como yo dije en clase, tengo mi esposo y dos hijos—Mike y Brad. Estoy muy feliz que tú estás en mi clase. Muy pronto vas a aprender inglés, y entonces puedes escribir usando inglés.

[You have one brother and one sister, your mother and father. You are very happy in your house. Your uncle and aunt came [come?] on Sundays. Is that what you told me? I have 2 brothers, 3 sisters, my father and mother. Also, as I said in class, I have my husband and two sons— Mike and Brad. I am very happy that you are in my class. Very soon you will learn English, and then you will be able to write in English.]

Mrs. Miller deciphered what Miguel seemed to be saying and responded in Spanish, first restating his message and then adding information about herself and encouraging him.

After the first few entries, Miguel began to mix the English words and phrases he was learning in with his Spanish. At times, when he wanted to communicate something important, he switched completely to Spanish and apologized. Mrs. Miller sometimes responded in Spanish and sometimes in English. Near the middle of September Miguel switched completely to English, a simple entry written with help from the classroom aide:

September 16

My name is Miguel. I'm from El Salvador. I'm ten years old. Today is Tuesday.

After that, much of Miguel's journal writing consisted of the repetition of English patterns similar to those he was working on in his workbook. Mrs. Miller often repeated the patterns and expanded them, adding new vocabulary and structures. (In an interview with Joy Peyton, Mrs. Miller said that she used that approach with all beginning English learners, to let them read familiar patterns while introducing new language.) In the interaction below, Miguel picked up on one of those structures to develop a new pattern.

September 20

Miguel: Today is Monday
My name is Miguel
You Mrs Miller my name is Miguel is student Mrs Miller is techer

Teacher: Today is Monday. Tomorrow will be Tuesday. You can write the days of the week. Miguel is a student. You are a boy. Do you like to watch TV?

Miguel: Today is Tuesday
I like to wach tus.
I like to study English
I like to pley football
I like to ken
I like to pteyl gan [play games]

By November, Mrs. Miller and Miguel began having actual conversations, still using simple structures. Mrs. Miller's writing provided a repetition of what Miguel had written, as well as new topics, words, and structures, which he then used freely in his entries. When she used words she thought would be new to him, she wrote them in both English and Spanish:

Teacher: I like Barcroft school.The people are very nice. The boys and girls are nice. Many people go to Barcroft school. Did you go to a big school in El Salvador?

Miguel: Yes meny pleople go to Barcroft Yes mi go in el salvador a big school meny people school in el salvador I like america to yuo like America

Teacher: Yes, I like America very much. What subjects (sujetos) did they teach you in El Salvador? Did you study (Estudiaste) math (matemáticas)? Did you study science (ciencia)? Did you study history (historia)?
In Barcroft school you study math. You study science. You study history. You study English.

Miguel: Yes stoti math in study science in study stori in English . . .

Miguel often reverted back to repeating fixed English patterns he knew, with vocabulary substitutions, but more and more he moved away from those patterns to more authentic language. Near the end of the year he began to discuss issues that were important to him.

May 4

   Miguel: . . . I want to go to summer school Mrs Miller my mother want to know how mush cost summer school I go with claudia to summer school Mrs Miller. . . .

   Teacher: Summer school for you costs $40.00 and for Claudia $34.00. All together it costs $74.00 for the 2 of you. You need to get the money and application in by the end of May.

   Miguel: Mrs Miller I bring the money . . . is very impoertant go to summer school.

May 12

   Miguel: . . . my sister is sad mrs. miller. be cast she not have friends in the claass.

   Teacher: I'm sorry Claudia is sad. There are many nice children in Dr. S____'s HILT class in the morning. Doesn't Claudia have friends there? Has she had any friends this year? Maybe she should talk to Dr. S____ or Mrs. W____. They could probably help her. Mrs. A____ could help her too.

   Miguel: maybe mrs. A____ help my sister for have friends mrs miller I sad too mrs miller. my sister want friends. . . .

It appears that the journal provided Miguel with a very important place to express himself and learn English. During certain class activities, when the teacher was working with the whole class or a group of students, the aide was busy, and Miguel wasn't working in his workbook, he seemed lost and stared out the window or drew pictures in a notebook. But when journal time came, he could participate. In the journal he could use the patterns he was working on in his workbook to actually communicate with another person who answered. While he was still manipulating those patterns in his workbook, he moved beyond them in his journal to authentic messages and structures.

It is impossible to know to what extent Mrs. Miller's role in the journal writing influenced Miguel's language and social development, but it appears that it was very important. Her writing, at his level and slightly beyond, served as a language "scaffold" (Cazden, 1983) on which he built his own writing. Her attention and the daily communication with her helped to promote his socialization. Several times he mentioned (in Spanish) his desire to be able to speak and write in English and his frustration that he wasn't doing better. She encouraged him, telling him how well he was doing. It seems that her attitudes, expressed in the journal, influenced his attitudes toward her class and school in general. After she had written several times how glad she was to have him in her class, he began to express his own happiness at being in her class and in school. At the end of the year Miguel wrote that he wanted to go to high school and get a good job, and he and Mrs. Miller reflected together about how much progress he had made since the beginning of the year. It is difficult to imagine, after watching Miguel in class for a year[7], where he would have gotten these opportunities for confidence and communication without the journal.

Larry: The Defeated Student Who Blossomed[8]

Larry, the son of migrant farm workers, entered the fifth grade already branded a failure. Like the other students in his class, who ranged from age 10 to 16, he spoke Spanish, his first language, at home and on the playground. His exposure to English came from television, the radio, and school. He was unable to read materials at his own grade level, wrote very little and, unless a turnaround occurred, would continue to fail in school and drop out by the time he reached junior high to work in the fields, following the crops from one region to another. Larry's development as a writer is encouraging, for it shows how a defeated student can be motivated to change his attitudes and performance, given the right conditions for reading and writing.

On the first day the students in Larry's class wrote in their dialogue journals, most turned in the minimum amount required, three lines of writing. Larry submitted a blank sheet of paper. His teacher wrote in his journal anyway asking, "How can I answer you if you don't write to me?" The next day Larry wrote:

> I like math because I can count by five and tens. I like to write about Bo & Be & I like to draw the pictures & write the . . .

His words trailed off, reflecting the years he had managed to stay in school doing very little writing. But the teacher responded:

---

[7]Joy Peyton did research for a year in this class.

[8]Larry's story is excerpted, with permission, from Hayes, Bahruth, and Kessler (1986) and informed by Hayes and Bahruth (1985).

I enjoy writing too. I also enjoy illustrating my stories when I finish. I also use pictures for ideas to write about. What problems bother you about writing?

Larry candidly answered:

Well, I can't not spell right. Thats what's bother me about writing.

After these initial, halting entries, Larry did start to write. His entries lengthened, and his topics included books he had been reading, his likes and dislikes, and poems that he particularly liked. He began to pose questions and answer the teacher's questions:

Teacher: Would you like to learn to play chess?

Larry: I taught that chess was lik checkers. But I no how to play checkers a lot. Have you play checkers & chinese checkers?

As he became more comfortable, confident, and secure with his writing, he began to write about his future:

Larry: I'm saying to my mom that I'm going to finish school and I am golling to college and study for a year and try for teacher because I like being a teacher.

Once he had filled the pages of his first journal, Larry asked whether he could begin another, adding, "do you remeber the frist day I didn't write guess like one line, I like writeing in my Journal."

This progress took time, but eventually Larry became a writer. With the rest of the class, he moved from the dialogue journal to many other kinds of writing, including history and science reports and contributions to books published within the class. Larry's teacher and the researchers working with his class believe that dialogue journal writing, which allows students to begin reading and writing where they are and in their own way, can serve as a catalyst to turn defeated students like Larry into readers and writers.

Janny: The "Good Student" and the Development of a Voice

Janny's family came to the United States from Vietnam when she was very young, so all of her schooling took place in the United States and her writing does not show features of a nonnative English speaker. However, her first and home language was Chinese and her family was active in the Vietnamese community in Los Angeles. We profile Janny because she represents a segment of students now in many classes in the United States—students from other countries who are bright, motivated, and determined to succeed. An examination of her writing during the year shows how a dialogue journal can provide such students with a voice. The journal becomes a place where they can reflect on what they are studying and learning as well as share freely their personal concerns and struggles with an interested adult, who serves as a model, but also participates as an equal in the sharing.

Janny was one of the top students in Leslee Reed's sixth grade class. She received among the highest scores in her class on the Reading and Math tests taken by all sixth graders in the school district at the end of the year. She was in the gifted program during her sixth grade year, was elected president of the class, was on the school council and drill team, was a school safety patrol, sang in the school chorus, and planned to play the violin in the orchestra in junior high.

At the beginning of the year Janny's journal entries were those of a good student who likes school and is eager to please. They were always neatly written and usually about school events and activities. They usually consisted of a brief review of the day's activities with a positive evaluation but little reflection or elaborating detail, as shown in this entry:

September 23

> Today in school we studied many things. In Geography we labeled places on the map. I finally got a chance to finish my name too. Every day when I have left the class I have realized that I have experienced and learned something new.

As Janny continued to write, she began to open up and express herself as an individual, writing much more than the three-sentence minimum, sometimes several pages, and giving her opinions on a variety of topics. Only parts of her entries are shown in the examples below. At times her opinions took the form of advice to the teacher or even complaints about what had happened in school. This is something that many of Mrs. Reed's students did in their journals once they had passed through what she considered to be rather boring, "model student" writing. It is also something she encouraged.

November 24

> Mrs. Reed, why don't you give grades? I think it would be a little bit better because then we would know how we're doing.

February 11

> I wish you would make the Spelling's Bee's a lot harder.

February 23

> The Spelling Bee we had today wasn't very good. It wasn't a real Spelling Bee it was more of a contest to see who could write faster.

Janny's opinions often extended beyond complaints to a variety of subjects, from the Presidential elections to the MX missile:

October 14

> Today we read a weekly reader about the M.X. Missile. Some people want it and some people don't. I don't like the idea.

November 4

> Today is election day and the polls are all going to be very busy. I certainly wish I knew who was going to win. I sure hope our new president will be a good one. I don't really care for any of the people who are running.

Most striking about Janny's journal is the level of sharing of opinions and ideas between her and Mrs. Reed. As they continued writing to each other, they developed a rapport that looked very much like a conversation between close friends. Sometimes this sharing revolved around personal topics:

December 12

> Janny: Have you put up a Christmas tree yet at your house? We haven't yet at mine. My mother says she thinks she'll get one today after all it's so close to christmas. My mother says that she thinks she likes a real christmas tree better than a fake on. I do like real christmas trees but I think it would be wiser to get a fake one. Artificial trees might cost a little more than real ones but they can last a whole lot longer.

> Teacher: No! I haven't put up a tree in my house yet. I hope to get it done this weekend. I agree with your Mother and insist on a fresh new tree. There is something about the smell and feel that I really enjoy. I do have some Christmas baking done!

But it also included topics the class was studying in school:

January 15

Teacher: Were you impressed with the time and energy it took Dr. Martin Luther King to get the world (and the U.S.) to understand that black people (and all people) have rights?

Janny: Yes I was impressed at how hard Mr. King worked so that his people could have rights like other people. He succeeded after a long time of hard work and he did not give up really surprised me!

Topics that Janny read or heard about:

May 22

Janny: Mrs. Reed do you think that plants have feelings? My father said that he thinks they do. He said that in the newspaper they had an article about an experiment at UCLA. Do you think that it could actually be true? I don't know what to think.

Teacher: Yes, I've read about experiments that show plants do respond to cruel words and actions by actually showing a kind of fear. They seem to respond to pleasant sounds and voices! I am inclined to think plants, like people, do better in a happy, pleasant environment.

Experiences outside of school:

February 17

Janny: Yesterday I want to the San Diego zoo. It was really fun.

Teacher: How lucky you were! The San Diego Zoo is such a great place to go! Did you go into the hummingbird house? It is one of my favorite places.

Janny: No, I didn't go into the hummingbird house. I don't think they have one. We had a map of the zoo and it didn't seem to have any place located for a hummingbird house. Anyway we went to the snake exhibitions. I was really surprised at the length of some of them and also the width of some of them too. There was one snake that was around 3 to 4 feet in length and there was a snake that was the length of this journal.

And plans for the future:

May 20

      Janny: If I am going to V I am going to be in the orchestra. I really love the things that the orchestra can do. I think it would even be better than the chorus.

    Teacher: It is fun to be in an orchestra! I played violin in orchestras for many years! You'd really love it. What instrument do you want to play? Are you taking music lessons now?

      Janny: It is such a coincidence because I was planning to play the violin or the flute in the orchestra. Both of them have very beautiful sounds. It really would be a pleasure to know how to play one. I haven't been taking music lessons but I hope I can be one of the beginners there.

During these discussions Mrs. Reed had the opportunity to display her tremendous enthusiasm for learning, and Janny, in response to this enthusiasm, seemed eager to share her own knowledge.

An important part of Mrs. Reed's class is reading for pleasure. Each day she reads part of a book aloud to the class and talks about books by the same author. There is time for silent reading of self-chosen books during which she reads as well. A reading specialist comes in several times during the year to talk about books, and the room is filled with books. Even though students are not asked to write about their reading in their journals, many do. Janny and Mrs. Reed had conversations in their journal about their reading that resemble those Nancie Atwell (1987) has with her junior high students in reading journals. These are clearly conversations between two people who enjoy and value reading.

November 14

      Janny: I'm reading the last edition of "The Great Brain." I can see why you really like the books. they are very interesting and exciting.

    Teacher: One of the reasons I enjoy the *Great Brain* series is because you get some ideas about the way life was during those years. We can't imagine life without indoor plumbing and lots of schools close to home. When you read those books you get some ideas about the way people lived then.

January 28

> Janny: I finished reading another one of Enid Blyton's books called fall into adventure. It was very exciting. Enid Blyton books are just the best books that I ever read.

> Teacher: It is interesting to read several books by the same author, isn't it? You sort of learn their style so you have an idea what to expect! I don't think I've read that one.

March 12

> Janny: I really have enjoyed reading the Phantom Tollbooth. It would go under "fantasies" wouldn't it. It really is funny and it makes the reader actually feel as if they were really the main character. Have you read the book? I guess you already have because you told me what it was like. I don't think that I've every enjoyed a book more.

> Teacher: I'm so pleased that you like *Phantom Tollbooth*! It is one of my very favorite books. I never read it that I don't have to laugh out loud. The play on words and the humor really amuse me.

Janny, like many girls her age in Mrs. Reed's class, wrote in her journal about conflicts with other girls in the class, often over who was "best friend" with whom and how her friends were treating her. At one point she had a falling out with her best friend, the other top student in the class, also from China. During the several weeks that this problem lasted Janny vented her feelings, and Mrs. Reed tried to offer understanding and encouragement.

May 1

> Janny: I'm feeling quite down in the dumps today. Guess who's putting me there. You're right Lisa and Sophia. Oh I'm so misearble I could cry. In fact I did start crying at the beginning of class but I stopped myself. If I didn't, I would have had tears streaming down my face. And also at a very fast rate. . . .

> Teacher: I am not surprised! You've been so calm and serene outwardly that inside you must be in a big turmoil. You have handled your feelings extremely well, but you are human! To cry . . . is natural and would release a lot of pressure which you've felt. The misunderstanding with Sophia and the pressure of the spelling bee is much too much.

> I had the feeling this afternoon that the problem was being worked out! Could it be?

Finally, through the journal, Janny was able to work through a problem that is common to high-achieving students—envy from others in the class. The class's regular spelling bees were very important to her; she was a good speller and usually won. At one point students from Mrs. Reed's class were chosen to compete in a schoolwide spelling bee, the winners of which would represent the school in a district-wide competition. Janny was excited and nervous about this competition, and wrote about it often in her journal.

February 27

> Mrs. Reed I hope you will tell us who's going to be in the Spelling Bee on Monday. I'm straining my nerves. I am just so nervous about it that I don't think I can stand it any longer. I was looking forward to it for so long. . . .

She was chosen as one of the contestants from her class, wrote about her excitement for several days, and won the spelling bee, meaning that she would represent the school on April 29. However, the victory was not a happy one. In the journal she expressed her frustration, and Mrs. Reed supported and encouraged her.

March 5

> Janny: I feel wierd. I don't know why. I don't really want to compete on April 29. I think I've had enough of Spelling Bees no matter how exciting they've been. I wonder if I can win? . . . Do you know someone named Maria G? Well you gave me the word "beginner" and I spelled it correctly so I won. Well Maria says that you just gave me the word because you wanted to. I know that's not true because I saw you pick out the word from the basket. . . . I wish that I didn't win the Spelling Bee. I know I should be happy about winning but I feel worse than I ever did. I don't care if I cry too much or what but I have to anyway. I feel very much as if the whole world is against me. Even what I thought were my best of friends. The people I trusted now hate me. Why can't they understand?

> Teacher: It is difficult to understand—and I understand and share your weird feelings! Do cry if you feel like it! You are human, your feelings are hurt and you are not at fault.

It is very disturbing. It is most difficult to be a good loser! Somehow being a loser you feel better if you can criticize or "tear down" the winner. The act of destroying the winner makes a poor loser feel better. Being a winner always puts you in the position of being a target for anyone who feels insecure or inferior.

You must try to win in April! I have great confidence in you—as do all of the other teachers here at Alexandria! You may not win, you may win, I don't know which. I do know you will do your very best to do honor to yourself and to your school. You are too fine a person to do otherwise!

I've read and answered most of the journals of our class already this evening. Almost all have been proud of you and angry that others were being mean.

Students like Janny, who enjoy school, excel in all aspects of it, and are not struggling with the basics of English, need a place to discuss their interests with someone who understands them and can expand their thinking. Janny and several other of the top students in her class (see Staton, 1989, for a profile of another student, from the Philippines) took advantage of the opportunity the journal provided them to work through, with Mrs. Reed, very important personal issues as well as things they were learning both in and out of school.

* * * * * *

These student profiles make one point very clear: Dialogue journals can be used in almost any program, with almost anyone. Whether students start out drawing or labelling pictures, writing lists of words, or writing extended and thoughtful texts, they can keep and benefit from a dialogue journal. The teacher benefits as well, for the permanent record of writing gives a rich, ongoing picture of students' development as individuals, thinkers, and writers.

CHAPTER 9

CONCLUSION
STUDYING DIALOGUE JOURNAL WRITING

A Reflection by Joy Peyton

My first introduction to dialogue journal writing was in 1980, when Jana Staton and Roger Shuy asked me to join them in their study of dialogue journals in Leslee Reed's sixth grade class of native English speakers. As the Research Assistant, my job was to number the journal pages and interactions, while at the same time reading the journals and taking notes on what I observed. I therefore had the luxury of poring over the lives and thoughts of 26 individuals as they moved through the school year (they had all given permission for us to study and write about their writing), and I was fascinated. I watched Joan complain about and fight against almost everything that happened that year but also stay in class. She was never kicked out of class and never sent to the office, routine events in her previous school years. I watched Tai work through what it meant to be a responsible young woman and student and handle her temper and emotions so she could think and work productively. I watched Gordon deal with the intricacies and difficulties of math and eventually move from frustration to love of it. (These stories are told in detail in Staton et al., 1988.) Mrs. Reed told us, and we came to believe, that the dialogue journals were the keystone of her teaching. This was where the battles were fought and a great deal of learning was done—not only about school subjects, but about life and growing up.

In 1981 Mrs. Reed was transferred to another school in which 65% of the students, and nearly all of the students in her class, were nonnative English speakers. We all wondered if the journals would "work." How could she write with students who didn't really know English? At the end of the year we collected, numbered, and read those journals, and

were fascinated again. Yes, they were genuine dialogues; they had
worked; but in some ways they were very different. These students
didn't complain very much, at least at the beginning of the year,
unlike the native English speakers. Instead, they asked question, after
question, after question: "Where are you from?" "How old are you?"
"Do we have school next week?" "What is Geography?" "What does
'equator' mean?" They wrote about their countries and their experiences adjusting to their new culture and language. These students
were attempting to work out meanings on many, many levels, and
again we followed them through the year as they did that. (The stories
of some of these students are told in Peyton & Staton, in press.)

An interesting thing happened when we started to talk about these
journals in workshops and at conferences in the early 1980s. At first
there was a certain amount of questioning of the whole idea—"Why
should students who are just learning English be allowed to write
about whatever they want to? What good is that kind of activity?"
"There are so many errors, and the teacher doesn't correct them.
How will these students ever learn English if their errors are not
corrected?" "Who has time for that sort of thing? We have a detailed
curriculum to cover." Of course, all of us have learned a great deal
since then about language acquisition, writing development, and
learning in general, and open-ended reading and writing activities
like dialogue journal writing have become more the norm than the
strange or threatening exception.

Since those days many more teachers have decided to incorporate
dialogue journals into their work, and I have had the privilege of
talking to and spending time in the classrooms of many dialogue
journal teachers and students. Over and over as I have observed and
listened, I have been struck by the importance of the three dynamics
that Mary Ellen Giacobbe and Nancie Atwell have talked about: time,
ownership, and response (cf. Atwell, 1987, pp. 54–72).

To do any significant writing, in dialogue journals or elsewhere,
students need *time*—time to think, plan, talk with others, or just gaze
out the window. The most stimulating classes I have been in have
been those in which there was plenty of time to write (and read).
Naveed, in Ruth Sedei's first grade class, at first took nearly all of the
reading and writing time available (at least two hours each day) to
read and write in his journal. That's how long he needed. As time
went on he, like the other students in his class, integrated his journal
writing with his other reading and writing, but he still decided himself
how much time to spend on it. In Mrs. Reed's sixth grade class Ben
kept his journal with him all day and wrote whenever he could—
during breaks, during lunch, after school, when he had finished his
other work. Of course, most students in Naveed's and Ben's classes

didn't need nearly as much time as Naveed and Ben did, but the fact that the students themselves determined the amount of time they would spend writing was important. Most ESL classes, however, last for less than an hour and don't have the luxury of long reading and writing times. But even in these classes there can be a quiet period in which students are free to put down their thoughts without hearing the teacher's voice or following the school's rigorous plan.

When we feel a sense of *ownership*, we take responsibility. Students who know they will read and write regularly begin to take ownership of that time. The students I have observed who felt they owned their journals and their writing time rarely needed to be reminded to get the journals out. They came into the room, got their journal, and began reading and writing or talking quietly, sharing parts of an entry with another student. First graders in Mrs. Sedei's class sometimes brought in bits of paper on which they had written words they wanted to use or beginnings of entries. They knew they would be writing, so had thought about their topics and gathered their resources. When I asked Gabriela if I could take a completed journal home to copy, she made me promise I would return it the next day, because she used it as a basis for her writing. The students in Kelly Miller's fourth through sixth grade class felt they were each writing a book collaboratively with Mrs. Miller, the story of their life for that year. Many talked about how they would read that book years later.

We have only recently realized the importance of *response* for developing language and writing. Not correction, but a real response that appreciates, contributes, extends, questions, critiques. A response that takes our thoughts and verbal creations seriously, stimulates us to continue them and helps us to take them still further. When a response is consistent and predictable, students begin responding themselves and a true dialogue is established, in which both participants benefit.

Professional writers have known for years how essential time, ownership, and response are for the success of their writing. Fortunately, we are discovering that they are also essential for students learning English, no matter what their age or language ability. Dialogue journal writing is one way to assure that these dynamics are operating in the classroom.

REFERENCES

Applebee, A. N. (1984). *Contexts for learning to write*. Norwood, NJ: Ablex.

Atwell, N. (1984). Writing and reading literature from the inside out. *Language Arts, 61*(3), 240–252.

Atwell, N. (1987). *In the middle: Writing, reading, and learning with adolescents*. Upper Montclair, NJ: Boynton/Cook.

Auerbach, E., & McGrail, L. (in press). Rosa's challenge: Connecting classroom and community contexts. In E. Auerbach (Ed.), *ESL in America: Myths and possibilities in linguistic minority education*. Boynton/Cook.

Bailes, C., Searles, S., Slobodzian, J., & Staton, J. (1986). *It's your turn now: A handbook for teachers of deaf students*. Washington, DC: Gallaudet University.

Borasi, R., & Rose, B. (in press). Journal writing and mathematics instruction. *Educational Studies in Mathematics*.

Brinton, C., & Holten, C. (1989). What novice teachers focus on: The practicum in TESL. *TESOL Quarterly, 23*(2), 343–350.

Bruner, J. (1966). *Toward a theory of instruction*. Cambridge, MA: Harvard University Press.

Calkins, L. M. (1986). *The art of teaching writing*. Portsmouth, NH: Heinemann.

Cazden, C. (1983). Adult assistance to language development: Scaffolds, models and direct instruction. In R. Parker & F. Davis (Eds.), *Developing literacy: Young children's use of language* (pp. 3–18). Newark, DE: International Reading Association.

Cummins, J. (1986). Empowering minority students: A framework for intervention. *Harvard Educational Review, 56*(1), 18–36.

Davis, F. (1983). Why you call me emigrant?: Dialogue journal writing with migrant youth. *Childhood Education, 60*(2), 110–116.

Dialogue, a newsletter about dialogue journals and other types of interactive writing. Washington, DC: Center for Applied Linguistics.

Farley, J. (1986). Analysis of written dialogue of educable mentally retarded writers. *Education and Training of the Mentally Retarded, 21*(3), 181–191.

Flores, B. M., & García, E. (1984). A collaborative learning and teaching experience using journal writing. *NABE Journal, 8*(2), 67–83.

Flores, B. M., Rueda, R., & Porter, B. (1986). Examining assumptions and instructional practices related to the acquisition of literacy with bilingual special education students. In A. C. Willig & H. F. Greenberg (Eds.), *Bilingualism and learning disabilities: Policy and practice for teachers and administrators*. New York: American Library Publishing Co.

Genishi, C. (1989). Observing the second language learner: An example of teachers' learning. *Language Arts, 66*(5), 509–515.

Hall, N., & Duffy, R. (1987). Every child has a story to tell. *Language Arts, 64*(5), 523–529.

Hayes, C. W., & Bahruth, R. (1985). Querer es poder. In J. Hansen, T. Newkirk, & D. Graves (Eds.), *Breaking ground: Teachers relate reading and writing in the elementary school* (pp. 97–108). Portsmouth, NH: Heinemann.

Hayes, C. W., Bahruth, R., & Kessler, C. (1986, September). The dialogue journal and migrant education. *Dialogue, 3*(3), 3–5.

Heath, S. B., & Branscombe, A. (1984). "Intelligent writing" in an audience community: Teacher, students, and researcher. In S. W. Freedman (Ed.), *The acquisition of written language: Revision and response* (pp. 3–32). Norwood, NJ: Ablex.

Hester, J. (1986, September). Features of semi-literate writing: One student's development. *Dialogue, 3*(3), 5–7.

Jones, P. (1988). *Knowing opportunities: Some possible benefits and limitations of dialogue journals in adult second language instruction*. Unpublished Masters' thesis, School for International Training, Brattleboro, VT.

Kessler, C. (1989, September). Interactive writing in content areas: A promising practice for all learners. *Dialogue, 6*(2), 2–4.

Kitagawa, M. M., & Kitagawa, C. (1987). *Making connections with writing*. Portsmouth, NH: Heinemann.

Klos, L. (1988, April). Dialogue journal entries as problem-posing codes. *Dialogue, 5*(11), 10–11.

Kreeft, J., Shuy, R. W., Staton, J., Reed, L., & Morroy, R. (1984). *Dialogue writing: Analysis of student-teacher interactive writing in the learning of English as a second language* (National Institute of Education Grant No. NIE-G-83-0030). Washington, DC: Center for Applied Linguistics. (ERIC Document Reproduction Service No. ED 252 097)

Loban, W. (1986). Research currents: The somewhat stingy story of research into children's language. *Language Arts, 63*(6), 608–616.

MacDonald, M. (1989). Oral dialogue journals: Spoken language in a communicative context. *TESL Reporter, 22*(2), 27–31.

Martin, J. (1989, September). Some practical suggestions for dialogue journals in the foreign language classroom. *Dialogue, 6*(2), 17–19.

McGuire, B. (1986). Where does the teacher intervene with underachieving writers? (ERIC Document Reproduction Service No. ED 285 193)

Naiman, D. W. (1988). *Telecommunications and an interactive approach to literacy in disabled students.* New York: New York University.

Pesola, C. A., & Curtain, H. (1989, September). A rationale for starting and managing dialogue journal writing in the foreign language class. *Dialogue, 6*(2), 16 & 17.

Peyton, J. K. (Ed.). (1990a). *Students and teachers writing together: Perspectives on journal writing.* Alexandria, VA: Teachers of English to Speakers of Other Languages.

Peyton, J. K. (1990b). Beginning at the beginning: First grade ESL students learn to write. In A. M. Padilla, H. H. Fairchild, & C. M. Valadez (Eds.), *Bilingual education: Issues and strategies* (pp. 195–218). Newbury Park, CA: Sage Publications.

Peyton, J. K., & Seyoum, M. (1989). The effect of teacher strategies on students' interactive writing: The case of dialogue journals. *Research in the Teaching of English, 23* (3), 310–334.

Peyton, J. K., & Staton, J. (in press). *Dialogue journals in the multilingual classroom: Building language fluency and writing skills through written interaction.* Norwood, NJ: Ablex.

Peyton, J.K., & Steinberg, R.R. (1985, May). "I can write!" Written interactions of mentally handicapped students. *Dialogue, 2*(4), 3–5.

Popkin, D. (1985). Dialogue journals: A way to personalize communication in a foreign language. *Foreign Language Annals, 18*(2), 153–156.

Raimes, A. (1984). Anguish as a second language: Remedies for composition teachers. In S. McKay (Ed.), *Composing in a second language* (pp. 81–96). Rowley, MA: Newbury House.

Reed, L. (1988). Dialogue journals make my whole year flow: The teacher's perspective. In J. Staton, R. W. Shuy, J. K. Peyton, & L. Reed, *Dialogue journal communication: Classroom, linguistic, social and cognitive views* (pp. 56–72). Norwood, NJ: Ablex.

Roderick, J. (1986). Dialogue writing: Context for reflecting on self as teacher and researcher. *Journal of Curriculum and Supervision, 1*(14), 305–315.

Roderick, J., & Berman, L. (1984). Dialoguing about dialogue journals: Teachers as learners. *Language Arts, 61*(7), 686–692.

Rose, B. (1989). Writing and mathematics: Theory and practice. In P. Connolly & T. Vilardi (Eds.), *Writing to learn mathematics and science* (pp. 15–30). New York: Teachers College Press.

Samway, K. D. (1989, March). Teachers and students as literary pen pals: An odyssey. Paper presented at the Twenty-third Annual TESOL Convention. San Antonio, TX.

Sayers, D. (1986a, December). Interactive writing with computers: One solution to the time problem. *Dialogue, 3*(4), 9–10.

Sayers, D. (1986b). Sending messages: Across the classroom and around the world. *TESOL Newsletter* [Supplement on computer-assisted language learning], *20*(1), 7–8.

Shor, I. (1986, Spring). An interview with Ira Shor. *Literacy Research Center Newsletter, 2*(1), 1–5.

Smith, F. (1983). *Essays into literacy.* Portsmouth, NH: Heinemann.

Smith, F. (1985). *Reading without nonsense* (second edition). New York: Teachers College Press.

Staton, J. (1985). Using dialogue journals for developing thinking, reading, and writing with hearing impaired students. *Volta Review, 7*(5), 127–154.

Staton, J. (1987, September). Opportunities for genuine communication at the secondary level. *Dialogue, 4*(2), 4–7.

Staton, J. (1989, September). "Speaking of fireballs": The playing fields of the mind. *Dialogue, 6*(2), 12–14.

Staton, J., Shuy, R. W., Peyton, J. K., & Reed, L. (1988). *Dialogue journal communication: Classroom, linguistic, social and cognitive views.* Norwood, NJ: Ablex.

Steffensen, M. S. (1986, March). The dialogue journal: A method for increasing cross-cultural reading comprehension. Paper presented at the Twentieth Annual TESOL Convention. Anaheim, CA.

Steffensen, M. S. (1987, April). The emergence of syntactic and semantic structures in L2 dialogue journals. Paper presented at the Annual Convention of the International Association of Applied Linguistics. Sydney, Australia.

Steffensen, M. S. (1988). The dialogue journal: A method for improving cross-cultural reading comprehension. *Reading in a Foreign Language, 5*(1), 193–203.

Taylor, D. (1988, March). Reading dialogue journals. Paper presented at the Twenty-second Annual TESOL Convention. Chicago, IL.

Urzúa, C. (1986, April). I grow for a living. Paper presented at the Twentieth Annual TESOL Convention. Anaheim, CA.

Urzúa, C. (1987). You stopped too soon: Second language children composing and revising. *TESOL Quarterly, 21*(2), 279–304.

Walworth, M. (1985). Dialogue journals in the teaching of reading. *Teaching English to Deaf and Second Language Students, 3*(1), 21–25.

Walworth, M. (1990). Interactive teaching of reading: A model. In J. K. Peyton (Ed.), *Students and teachers writing together: Perspectives on journal writing* (pp. 35–47). Alexandria, VA: Teachers of English to Speakers of Other Languages.

APPENDIX

FURTHER READING

There is extensive material available for the teacher desiring to know more about dialogue journal use and research. Although not all of it focuses on limited English proficient students, the approaches and findings are in most cases generalizable to them.

For those wishing to conduct **TEACHER TRAINING WORK-SHOPS** on the use of dialogue journal writing, a workshop packet is available, designed to be used along with this handbook. It includes detailed guidelines for conducting the workshop, over 30 samples of student writing that can be made into overhead transparencies, background materials for the presenter, and handouts. The packet is available from the Center for Applied Linguistics, 1118–22nd St. N.W., Washington, DC 20037, attn: *Dialogue.*

A **NEWSLETTER** called *Dialogue* was published three times a year from 1982 to 1989. In it, teachers and researchers describe their uses of dialogue journals and research related to their use. Back issues are available from the Center for Applied Linguistics, attn: *Dialogue.*

Two **TEACHER HANDBOOKS** focus on the use of dialogue journals with deaf students: *It's Your Turn Now: A Handbook for Teachers of Deaf Students.* Cindy Bailes, Susan Searls, Jean Slobodzian, and Jana Staton. 1986. Washington, D.C.: Gallaudet University (focusing on elementary schools). Available from Outreach PreCollege Program, KDES, PAS6, 800 Florida Avenue, NE, Washington, DC 20002; and *Conversations in writing: A guide to using dialogue journals with deaf post-secondary and secondary students.* Jana Staton, Ed. 1980. Washington, DC: Gallaudet University. Available from the Gallaudet Research Institute, Gallaudet University, 800 Florida Avenue, NE, Washington, DC 20002.

A **BOOK** describing research and practice with both personal and dialogue journal writing, with nonnative English speakers, primarily adults, is also available from Teachers of English to Speakers of Other

119

Languages: *Students and teachers writing together: Perspectives on journal writing.* Joy Kreeft Peyton (Ed.). 1990.

There are also numerous other books and articles about dialogue journal writing. They are divided here into overall categories of interest.

Books and Articles

Dialogue journal use with various student populations

General - with any students

Kreeft, Joy. (1984). Dialogue writing: Bridge from talk to essay writing. *Language Arts, 61*(2), 141–150.

Lindfors, Judith Wells. (1988). From "talking together" to "being together in talk." *Language Arts, 65*(2), 135–141.

Sayers, Dennis. (1986, December). "Interactive" writing with computers: One solution to the time problem. *Dialogue, 3*(4), 9–10.

Shuy, Roger W. (1984, summer). Language as a foundation for education: The school context. *Theory Into Practice,* 167–174.

Shuy, Roger W. (1987). Research currents: Dialogue as the heart of learning. *Language Arts, 64*(8), 890–897.

Staton, Jana. (1983, March). Dialogue journals: A new tool for teaching communication. *ERIC/CLL News Bulletin,* pp. 1–6.

Staton, Jana. (1987). The power of responding in dialogue journals. In Toby Fulwiler (Ed.), *The journal book.* Portsmouth, NH: Boynton/Cook.

Staton, Jana. (1988). ERIC/RCS report: Dialogue journals. *Language Arts, 65*(2), 198–201.

Staton, Jana, & Shuy, Roger W. (1988). Talking our way into writing and reading: Dialogue journal practice. In B. A. Raforth & D. L. Rubin (Eds.), *The social construction of written communication* (pp. 195–217). Norwood, NJ: Ablex.

Staton, Jana, Shuy, Roger W., Peyton, Joy K., & Reed, L. (1988). *Dialogue journal communication: Classroom, linguistic, social and cognitive views.* Norwood, NJ: Ablex.

With nonnative English speaking students

Lindfors, Judith Wells. (1988). From helping hand to reciprocity to mutuality: Dialogue journal writing with Zulu students. *Journal of Learning, 1*(1), 63–85.

Lindfors, Judith Wells. (1988). Zulu students' questioning in dialogue journals. *Questioning Exchange, 2*(3), 289–304.

Peyton, Joy Kreeft. (1986, Fall). Interactive writing: Making writing meaningful for language minority students. *NABE News*, 19–21.

Peyton, Joy Kreeft. (1990). Dialogue journal writing and the acquisition of English grammatical morphology. In J. K. Peyton (Ed.), *Students and teachers writing together: Perspectives on journal writing* (pp. 67–97). Alexandria, VA: Teachers of English to Speakers of Other Languages.

Peyton, Joy Kreeft, & Seyoum, Mulugeta. (1989). The effect of teacher strategies on ESL students' writing: The case of dialogue journals. *Research in the Teaching of English, 23* (3), 310–334.

Peyton, Joy Kreeft, & Staton, Jana. (in press). *Dialogue journals in the multilingual classroom: Building language fluency and writing skills through written interaction.* Norwood, NJ: Ablex.

Sayers, Dennis. (1986). Sending messages: Across the classroom and around the world. *TESOL Newsletter* supplement on computer-assisted language learning, *20*(1), pp. 7–8.

Staton, Jana, Peyton, Joy Kreeft, & Gutstein, Shelley (Eds.). (1986, March). Dialogue journals in ESL settings [theme issue]. *Dialogue, 3*(2).

Staton, Jana, Peyton, Joy Kreeft, & Gutstein, Shelley (Eds.). (1988, December). Interactive writing in bilingual education [theme issue]. *Dialogue, 5*(3).

With migrant students

Davis, Fran. (1983). Why you call me emigrant?: Dialogue journal writing with migrant youth. *Childhood Education, 60*(2), 110–116.

Hayes, Curtis W., & Bahruth, Robert. (1985). Querer es poder. In J. Hansen, T. Newkirk, & D. Graves (Eds.), *Breaking ground: Teachers relate reading and writing in the elementary school* (pp. 97–108). Portsmouth, NH: Heinemann.

Staton, Jana, Peyton, Joy Kreeft, & Gutstein, Shelley (Eds.). (1986, September). Dialogue journals for developing literacy in refugee, migrant, and adult basic education [theme issue]. *Dialogue, 3*(3).

With deaf students

Albertini, John. (1990). Coherence in deaf students' writing. In J. K. Peyton (Ed.), *Students and teachers writing together: Perspectives on journal writing* (pp. 127–136). Alexandria, VA: Teachers of English to Speakers of Other Languages.

Albertini, John, & Meath-Lang, Bonnie. (1986). Analysis of student-teacher exchanges in dialogue journal writing. *Journal of Curriculum Theorizing, 7*, 1–14.

Cannon, Beverly, & Polio, Charlene. (1989). An analysis of input and interaction in the dialogue journals of deaf community college students. *Teaching English to Deaf and Second Language Students, 7*(1), 12–21.

Meath-Lang, Bonnie. (1990). The dialogue journal: Reconceiving curriculum and teaching. In J. K. Peyton (Ed.), *Students and teachers writing together: Perspectives on journal writing* (pp. 5–17). Alexandria, VA: Teachers of English to Speakers of Other Languages.

Staton, Jana. (1985). Using dialogue journals for developing thinking, reading, and writing with hearing-impaired students. *Volta Review, 7*(5), 127–154.

Staton, Jana, Peyton, Joy Kreeft, & Gutstein, Shelley (Eds.). (1987, December). Interactive writing in deaf education [theme issue]. *Dialogue, 4*(3).

Walworth, Margaret. (1990). Interactive teaching of reading: A model. In J. K. Peyton (Ed.), *Students and teachers writing together: Perspectives on journal writing* (pp. 35–47). Alexandria, VA: Teachers of English to Speakers of Other Languages.

With young children

Bode, Barbara A. (1989). Dialogue journal writing. *Reading Teacher, 42* (8), 568–571.

Braig, Deborah. (1986). Six authors in search of an audience. In Bambi Schieflen (Ed.), *The acquisition of literacy: Ethnographic perspectives* (pp. 110–113). Norwood, NJ: Ablex.

Britton, James. (1987). *Reading and writing in the classroom.* Berkeley, CA: Center for the Study of Writing.

Farley, Jack W., & Farley, Susan L. (1987). Interactive writing and gifted children: Communication through literacy. *Journal for the Education of the Gifted, 10*(2), 99–106.

Flores, Barbara, & García, Erminda A. (1984). A collaborative learning and teaching experience using journals. *NABE Journal, 8*(2), 67–83.

Hall, Nigel (Ed.). (1989). *Writing with reason: The emergence of authorship in young children* (selected chapters). Portsmouth, NH: Heinemann.

Hall, Nigel, & Duffy, Rose. (1987). Every child has a story to tell. *Language Arts, 64*(5), 523–529.

Kitagawa, Mary, & Kitagawa, Chisato. (1987). Journal writing. In M. M. Kitagawa & C. Kitagawa (Eds.), *Making connections with writing: An expressive writing model in Japanese schools* (pp. 58–66). Portsmouth, NH: Heinemann.

Peyton, Joy Kreeft. (1990). Beginning at the beginning: First grade ESL students learn to write. In A. M. Padilla, H. H. Fairchild, & C. M. Valadez (Eds.), *Bilingual education: Issues and strategies* (pp. 195–218). Newbury Park, CA: Sage Publications.

Staton, Jana. (1984). Thinking together: Interaction in children's reasoning. In C. Thaiss & C. Suhor (Eds.), *Speaking and writing, K–12* (pp. 144–187). Champaign, IL: National Council of Teachers of English.

Staton, Jana, Peyton, Joy Kreeft, & Gutstein, Shelley (Eds.). (1989, April). Interactive writing in elementary education [theme issue]. *Dialogue*, *6*(1).

With special needs students

Farley, Jack W. (1986). Analysis of written dialogue of educable mentally retarded writers. *Education and Training of the Mentally Retarded, 21*(3), 181–191.

Farley, Jack W., & Farley, Susan L. (1987). Interactive writing and gifted children: Communication through literacy. *Journal for the Education of the Gifted*, *10*(2), 99–106.

Flores, Barbara, Rueda, Robert, & Porter, Brenda. (1986). Examining assumptions and instructional practices related to the acquisition of literacy with bilingual special education students. In A. C. Willig & H. F. Greenberg (Eds.), *Bilingualism and learning disabilities: Policy and practice for teachers and administrators*. New York: American Library Publishing Co.

Goldman, Susan, & Rueda, Robert. (1988). Developing writing skills in bilingual exceptional children. *Exceptional Children*, *54*(6), 543–551.

Staton, Jana, Peyton, Joy Kreeft, & Gutstein, Shelley (Eds.). (May, 1985). Dialogue journals with students with special needs [theme issue]. *Dialogue*, *2*(4).

With teachers in teacher education

Brinton, Donna, & Holten, Christine. (1989). What novice teachers focus on: The practicum in TESL. *TESOL Quarterly*, *23*(2), 343–350.

Fishman, Andrea, R., & Rover, Elizabeth J. (1989). "Maybe I'm just *not* teacher material": Dialogue journals in the student teaching experience. *English Education*, *21* (2), 92–109.

Flores, Barbara M., & García, Erminda A. (1984). A collaborative learning and teaching experience using dialogue journal writing. *NABE Journal*, *8*(2), 67–83.

Roderick, Jessie. (1986). Dialogue writing: Context for reflecting on self as teacher and researcher. *Journal of Curriculum and Supervision, 1*(4), 305–315.

Roderick, Jessie, & Berman, Louise. (1984). Dialoguing about dialogue journals: Teachers as learners. *Language Arts*, *61*(7), 686–692.

Staton, Jana, Peyton, Joy Kreeft, & Gutstein, Shelley (Eds.). (1988, September). Interactive writing in teacher education [theme issue]. *Dialogue*, *5*(2).

Dialogue journals and writing

Farr, Marcia, & Janda, Mary Ann. (1985). Basic writing students: Investigating oral and written language. *Research in the Teaching of English, 19*(1), 62–83.

Kreeft, Joy. (1984). Dialogue writing: Bridge from talk to essay writing. *Language Arts, 61*(2), 141–150.

Peyton, Joy Kreeft. (1986). Literacy through written interaction. *Passage: A Journal for Refugee Education, 2*(1), 24–29. (ERIC Document Reproduction Service No. ED 273 097)

Peyton, Joy Kreeft, Staton, Jana, Richardson, Gina, & Wolfram, Walt. (1990). The influence of writing task on ESL students' written production. *Research in the Teaching of English, 24*(2), 142–171.

Staton, Jana. (1981, October). Literacy as an interactive process. *The Linguistic Reporter*, pp. 1–5.

Dialogue journals and reading

Atwell, Nancie. (1984). Writing and reading literature from the inside out. *Language Arts, 61*(3), 240–252.

Atwell, Nancie. (1987). *In the middle: Writing, reading, and learning with adolescents.* Upper Montclair, NJ: Boynton/Cook.

Gambrell, Linda B. (1985). Dialogue journals: Reading-writing interaction. *The Reading Teacher, 38*(6), pp. 512–515.

Staton, Jana. (1986). The teacher's writing as text. *Greater Washington Reading Council Journal, 11*, 3–4.

Steffensen, Margaret S. (1988). The dialogue journal: A method for improving cross-cultural reading comprehension. *Reading in a Foreign Language, 5*(1), 193–203.

Walworth, Margaret. (1990). Interactive teaching of reading: A model. In J.K. Peyton (Ed.), *Students and teachers writing together: Perspectives on journal writing* (pp. 37–47). Alexandria, VA: Teachers of English to Speakers of Other Languages.

Dialogue journals and content-area instruction

Borasi, Raffaella, & Rose, Barbara J. (in press). Journal writing and mathematics instruction. *Educational Studies in Mathematics.*

Rose, Barbara J. (1989). Writing and mathematics: Theory and practice. In Paul Connolly and Teresa Vilardi (Eds.), *Writing to learn mathematics and science* (pp. 15–30). New York: Teachers College Press.

Staton, Jana, Peyton, Joy Kreeft, & Gutstein, Shelley (Eds.). (1989, September). Interactive writing in content-area instruction [theme issue]. *Dialogue, 6*(2).

Also available from TESOL

All Things to All People
Donald C. Flemming, Lucie C. Germer, and Christiane Kelley

A New Decade of Language Testing Research:
Selected Papers From the 1990 Language Testing Research Colloquium
Dan Douglas and Carol Chapelle, Editors

Books for a Small Planet:
An Intercultural Bibliography for Young English Language Learners
Dorothy S. Brown

Common Threads of Practice:
Teaching English to Children Around the World
Katharine Davies Samway and Denise McKeon, Editors

Dialogue Journal Writing with Nonnative English Speakers:
A Handbook for Teachers
Joy Kreeft Peyton and Leslee Reed

Dialogue Journal Writing with Nonnative English Speakers:
An Instructional Packet for Teachers and Workshop Leaders
Joy Kreeft Peyton and Jana Staton

Discourse and Performance of International Teaching Assistants
Carolyn G. Madden and Cynthia L. Myers, Editors

Diversity as Resource:
Redefining Cultural Literacy
Denise E. Murray, Editor

New Ways in Teacher Education
Donald Freeman, with Steve Cornwell, Editors

New Ways in Teaching Reading
Richard R. Day, Editor

New Ways in Teaching Speaking
Kathleen M. Bailey and Lance Savage, Editors

Students and Teachers Writing Together:
Perspectives on Journal Writing
Joy Kreeft Peyton, Editor

Video in Second Language Teaching:
Using, Selecting, and Producing Video for the Classroom
Susan Stempleski and Paul Arcario, Editors

For more information, contact

Teachers of English to Speakers of Other Languages, Inc.
1600 Cameron Street, Suite 300
Alexandria, Virginia 22314 USA
Tel 703-836-0774 • Fax 703-836-7864